Seeking Attention

T0348971

Seeking Attention

30 Ways of Being Present

by
Dominic Pettman

Published by Repeater Books

An imprint of Watkins Media Ltd

Unit 11 Shepperton House

89-93 Shepperton Road

London

N1 3DF

United Kingdom

www.repeaterbooks.com

A Repeater Books paperback original 2025

1

Distributed in the United States by Random House, Inc., New York.

ISBN: 9781915672674

Ebook ISBN: 9781915672711

Printed and bound by CPI Group (UK) Ltd, Croydon, CR0 4YY

Table of Contents

Introduction:
On Types, Traits, Characters, and Caricatures

Most of us, if pressed, would admit to having a "type." And this type is what forms the general outline of our romantic interest or aesthetic appeal. Perhaps we even have a suite of *different* types, depending on our mood, or time of life. Many of us also, by extension, eventually realize that we ourselves must also represent a type for others. And once we have this decisive realization, we comport ourselves accordingly — sometimes playing up to type, and other times surprising even ourselves by acting out of character (diverging, that is, from the *genus* with which we identify). No matter how unique we feel — no matter how singular — we are inevitably shepherded into various categories and asked to conform to specific groupings, according to the matrix of our characteristics, sensibilities, proclivities, and life decisions. For the purposes of cultural convenience, as well as social legibility, we often borrow a significant percentage of ourselves from previous, pre-established genres of personhood. This is a fancy way of saying we all have internalized role models, whether we acknowledge them or not. As a result, a substantial portion of our own identity can be described as "off the rack" (a truth signaled by the current popularity of the term "basic," used to refer to a type of factory-setting individual, an inveterate conformist to the fashions of the day). Western Europeans, ever attuned to existential wavelengths, often go so far as to call any random guy they happen to meet in the course of a day a "*type*" (French), "*typ*" (German), or "*tipo*" (Italian). (Although it's true that these *types* are usually people who present as male, female equivalents also exist, such as the "nana," in French.)

We are *all* types, in other words (just as we are all "randos"). And we all broadcast our various affiliations through social signals: some with meticulous forethought, others with almost instinctive disregard. Goths, for instance, are a cultural type, emerging nearly half a century ago, with roots in previous marginal, aestheticized formations. They announce their proud auto-typing by dressing in black, listening to the latest underground homages to the Cure, and having a generally depressive outlook on life. This is a type of human shorthand, used to make potential affiliations easier and clearer while signaling to others, "Don't bother — I'm not your type." Within the goth community, however, there are of course wildly diverging personalities and modes of expression. The same goes for any other type you can think of: spinster librarian, gamer bro, fabulous club kid, pedantic Ivy League professor, aloof supermodel, Asian "tiger mom," surly incel, social justice warrior, petrol head, e-girl, virulent anti-vaxxer, Southern good old boy, jaded detective, butch lesbian from the Pacific Northwest, and so on. The lens can be swapped for greater magnification, revealing intricate distinctions and ever more niche sub-types nested inside each other like animated Russian dolls. Conversely, we can zoom out to make room for the most broad-brush typology imaginable. (For instance, dividing the global population into twelve loose units allows us to describe more than 8 percent of all people on the planet as "such a Virgo.")

"We are all anagrams of each other," wrote Vladimir Nabokov. We tend, however, to gather in phonemic clusters: familiar groups that make us feel comfortable, provide a sense of belonging, or — if new to the fold — represent an aspirational thrill (all of which can lead to the dreaded "imposter syndrome," when we are too self-conscious about our credentials to feel worthy of inclusion). Through self-stereotyping, we hope we will be "seen," even though that kind of visibility comes at the cost of our singular personhood. We strategically lease a previously established *persona* in order to smooth access into specific worlds. We rewrite ourselves so that we read as "familiar enough" to "pass" as a public person according to an established set of traits or properties.

That said, the hipper the milieu, the more pressure there is to exhibit novel modes of presentation. A significant percentage of memes attest to this fact. Memes have become an efficient way of identifying and perpetuating *new* types, which in turn helps us get on with the constant business of what the sociologist Pierre Bourdieu simply called "distinction." Memes are, in other words, social sorting mechanisms. Along with dress codes, uniforms, tattoos, slang, vocal styles, initiation ceremonies, rites of passage, love languages, magazine quizzes, profile tags, and so on, there is no shortage of ways to encourage and demonstrate adhesion to something beyond yourself, something that nevertheless expresses an essential quality about your sense of self. Here we again encounter the irony that what feels most intimate to ourselves — that is to say, our private, personal selfhood — is in fact something that largely precedes us, and is bequeathed to us from outside, according to caprices and serendipities that are beyond our control. (According to a recent online survey, I myself am only 10 percent "yes Chad," but a much higher percentage "doomer girl.") The Marxist sociologist Louis Althusser called this "interpellation," the process whereby our identity is posited by an Other, someone with authority who "hails" our sense of self and station from afar. Through these inter-subjective dynamics, the "you" that we identify with is first born in the phrase, "Hey you!" — at least conceptually speaking. Today we are hailed as much by social media bots as we are by communal authority figures, complicating our relationship to ourselves.

Modern Moral Subjects

"Stereotypes" were originally the solid metal plates used in eighteenth-century printing machines to ensure uniformity in the typesetting process. The term was later applied to social types and caricatures, since these too churn out familiar, standardized images (albeit mental images, as a type of social currency). Stereotypes, in this more common understanding of the term, are versions of people we haven't met but *feel* that we have: variations on a limited human theme. Additionally, they are people we *have* met but who we couldn't see as individuals because we preferred to see them as merely the bearers of predictable cultural tics — the real-world puppets of prejudiced qualities. This connection to the printing press supports Marshall McLuhan's famous claim, more than half a century ago, that we ourselves are media artifacts — more so than the other way around.

Today, our frenetic and all-encompassing mediascape provides the tools, clothes, languages, aesthetics, gestures, and general models for our own pathway through the world (even if we reject the world almost completely, since in this inverse case we are then a *hikkomori* type — or an old-fashioned shut-in.) In to this highly mimetic existential economy — where we are all obliged to remind each other of people we've already encountered — our internal thoughts and feelings play second fiddle to our capacity to imitate familiar ways of being. (This is why it can be both fascinating and disconcerting when we encounter someone who can't easily be pigeonholed.) Eccentricity is tolerated, but only to a point, and only as an incubation chamber for new twists on the already known. To quote the protagonist from Nick Hornby's *High Fidelity*: "What really matters is what you like, not what you *are* like."

Social commentators and amateur anthropologists throughout the centuries have on occasion taken it upon themselves to take an inventory of some dominant types of their age, a process that combines satire, taxonomy, portraiture, group psychology, and vernacular sociology. Our first record of just such an attempt is the "character sketches" by the hand of Aristotle's successor, Theophrastus. In the fourth century BC, this early moral philosopher set about creating a catalogue of types, each one a lesson in how not to be a good person. As such, his examples included the boaster, the newsmonger, the flatterer, the chatterer, and the grumbler.

For subtle cultural reasons, associated primarily with literacy and national self-understanding, the French have historically been especially keen on social typology. In the second half of the seventeenth century, for instance, the philosopher Jean de La Bruyère published his famous book of "characters": a collection of types that one typically found at court, in the town square, and elsewhere, depicted also for the purposes of moral instruction. These included the coquette, the flatterer, the parvenu, the charitable man, the dolt, the glutton, and the "Narcissus." Speaking of the latter, La Bruyère writes:

> 'I have seen this man somewhere,' you'll say, 'and, though his face is familiar to me, I have forgotten where it was.' It is familiar to many other people, and, if possible, I will assist your memory. Was it on the Boulevard, in a carriage, or in the large alley of the Tuileries, or else in the dress-circle at the theatre? Was it at church, at a ball, or at Rambouillet; or, rather, can you tell me where you have not seen him, and where he is not to be met with? If some well-known criminal is going to be executed, or if there are any fireworks, he makes his appearance at a window at the town-hall; if someone enters the town in state, you see him in the reserved seats.

This man is familiar to the reader, even if he cannot be reduced to a single face or name. Indeed, he is a phalanx, a restless plurality. He is the oil painting ancestor of today's "that guy."

Around the same time, the playwright Molière added his own portraits to the mix, depicting on the French stage character types such as the misanthrope, the miser, and the hypochondriac. A century hence, the eccentric proto-socialist thinker Charles Fourier became obsessed with cataloging esoteric psycho-spiritual distinctions between people and matching them up in "passionate" utopian communities, like a one-man version of today's dating apps. Fourier was a born taxonomist, and was obsessed with making finer and finer divisions within the same overall categories; for instance, he recorded (and ranked!) at least forty-nine types of cuckold (including the imaginary cuckold, the sympathetic cuckold, and the bewitched cuckold). Balzac, for his part, decided to drill down and provide a taxonomy of civil servants and administrators in his book *The Bureaucrats*. Here we meet the dapper, the bootlicker, the drudge; components in "a physiology of the entire office system." Meanwhile, across the border in Germany, Franz Xaver Messerschmidt presented his own cast of characters, not with a pen, but with a sculptor's chisel. His three-dimensional stone portraits are strikingly modern looking, their expressive exuberance bordering on the grotesque. Confounding the mute dignity of official busts, Messerschmidt's often comic types include the yawner, the wag, the know-it-all, and even the "incapable bassoonist." Across the pond, English social painter William Hogarth also depicted common types in visual form: in his case, these were pictures, satirizing "modern moral subjects" like gin drinkers, harlots, and rakes. Charles Dickens, a century later, liked to keep himself amused indexing the real-life social caricatures he encountered in his daily rounds. These ended up in his *Sketches of Young Ladies, Young Gentlemen, and Young Couples*, no doubt also informing some of his most famous novelistic characters.

In the middle of the nineteenth century, journalists began noting new social sub-species emerging from the compressed recesses of the burgeoning cities, including the dandy, the bohemian, the vamp, and the flaneur. These would, in the following century, be followed by flappers, beatniks, hippies, punks, and rappers (to name only some of the most obvious). At the turn of the twentieth century, phrenologists claimed to have invented a science that could sort humans into moral categories according to the shape and size of their skulls — a racist and dubious logic that is alive and well today, coded into the digital fabric of facial recognition software, the same kind that erroneously presumes to be keeping our airports safe and our supermarkets free of shoplifters.

Observing this history from the vantage point of his Swiss facility, the mystically inclined psychologist Carl Jung went so far as to theorize the existence of archetypes lurking in the collective unconscious: metaphysical templates that actualize themselves in our stories and characters, as well as take flesh in our friends, family, and foes, no matter which time period or culture we belong to or which language we speak. These are indeed universally recognizable types, found in myths and legends around the world — as well as in the latest blockbuster movie or video game — including the hero, the lover, the trickster, and the sage. (As an aside, I should mention that I have Jung to thank for one of my former side-hustles, since — as a semiotician for hire — I was once asked to provide a comprehensive inventory of *new* archetypes, or "keno-types" as they came to be called, for a high-concept branding company. These archetypes 2.0 were mainly assembled for the purposes of selling fragrances and fashion to women of different... well... types. I seem to remember the "domestic goddess," "soulful siren," and "manic pixie dream girl"... though it must be noted that this was back in the aughts, and new types fade, and new ones are born, every few months. Indeed, according to today's trending hashtags, the highly influential "girl boss" is now being replaced by her anti-motivational niece, known as the "slug girl.")

Remaining faithful to my own type — broadly speaking, "aging Gen X cultural Marxist urbanite, of the basic white guy persuasion" — I feel compelled to take another tentative census of contemporary characters. Given how many of these exist in our fractalized, filter-bubble world, however, it is necessary to contain the process so it doesn't spiral out into infinity. And so, for the practical purposes of a book, I am limiting myself to thirty "portraits." Moreover, I am offering a guiding formula amid these observations, one that ties the actions of the individual to the group in which they belong, and which helps us make some sense of the static and noise of the echo-chamber present. This formula can be condensed to the following statement: "You are what you pay attention to."

The question of attention is a complex one, especially in an age defined by distraction, clickbait, ADHD, and the industrial engineering of millisecond parcels of micro-attention. We are not only living inside a ferocious "attention economy," as many have noted, but also a complex "attention ecology," one that informs everything we do, perceive, and rely on. I am, therefore, keen to record "typical" modes of attention, specific ways of being within Being itself, before many of these go extinct. In this sense, my project is both insanely grand and especially modest. It is grand in the sense that it suggests that any given portrait or character tells us a great deal about high-stakes elements of life: identity, purpose, vocation, meaning. The art of life. On the other hand, it is also very modest in recognizing that any effort toward this kind of census is necessarily just scratching the surface. Surprisingly, while the *Urban Dictionary* crowdsources definitions of neologisms, and various fan-wikis obsessively detail every minor character in beloved IP franchises, we don't yet seem to have a wiki of different cultural types. Such a resource or database would be a cultural analog to the Global Biodiversity Census: a record of millions of biological species, many of which have sadly ceased to exist even just a few years after they first stood up on six legs or more to be counted by the hapless, somewhat well-meaning humans.

Indeed, speaking of the non-human world, one striking thing occurred to me while detailing some of the specific types depicted in the following pages (that is, specific ways of paying attention). Any typology of our present moment must also include non-humans, since our precious capacity — praised by the philosophers since the beginning of writing — to focus on the world in full consciousness, and shared cognizance, is swiftly being outsourced to, or even outperformed by, our non-human neighbors. Computers are paying attention to the world in profound, unnerving, unfathomable ways. The explosion of AI in recent years reminds us that machine learning is outpacing human learning by nanoseconds and gigaflops (even as human learning seems to have stalled, if not started devolving). Not only that, our ethological sciences are now advanced enough to admit in public that animals are better at paying attention to the world than we are, and have been all this time, with more sophistication, sensitivity, and perhaps even intelligence. So it can be a humbling experience to really follow the logic that "you are what you pay attention to" when the "you" in this sentence can also be a dog, or a whale, or an avatar, or a chatbot, as much as a chef, or a critic, or a dancer, or an airline pilot.

In other words, things may not be as simple as the critics of our current mediascape make them out to be,when they claim that attention is a precious resource that is beginning to dwindle and dry up, in a hyper-distracted world. Perhaps there is, counter-intuitively, *more* attention than ever. But this attention is being fracked, fractured, fragmented, as well as solicited, manufactured, and even off-loaded on to bots and bits, algorithms and microsensors. Such is the arc, and provocation, I try to follow in my thirty portraits of attention within.

Not My Type

Before meeting my characters, however, I'd like to establish one last idea, and that is the fact that identity construction is just as much a negative operation as a positive one. This is to say, we figure out who we are, or who we want to be, by reacting *against* other forms of being or other ways of doing things. "You are what you eat," goes the old saying. But it's just as accurate to say that "you are what you *don't* eat." This is why the English call the French "frogs" when they want to be rude: the implication being that it would compromise one's British heritage and identity — even citizenship — to partake of *cuisses de grenouilles* rather than steak-and-kidney pie. (At the very least, eating frogs' legs would suggest that you didn't vote for Brexit and are thus suspect from a dominant, ethno-sentimentalist perspective.) Freud called this fundamental human foible "the narcissism of minor differences." And this is why there are often fierce identity clashes between types that are, to outsiders, very similar: the Sunnis and the Shi'ites, the Catholics and the Protestants, Yankees fans and Red Socks fans, the Mods and the Rockers. Why can't they all get along, given each pair is fundamentally the same kind of person? They are all Muslims, or Christians, or baseball fans, or music fans. And yet we seem to organize intensified energies of identity around vanishingly slight forms of difference.

Some of these narcissisms of minor differences are exquisitely baroque in the degree to which they will make distinctions. In New York, for instance, there have been riots between different factions of Hasidic Jews. I'm also told that every conference dedicated to the work of Jacques Lacan breaks down into furtive cliques according to which specific lecture series attendees have adopted as their key gateway to the gnomic thinker's universe. (Choose wisely, lest you have to sit at the losers' table during the lunch break, like in *Mean Girls*.) Such are the ways, and pressures, that create the contours of our selfhood when it is drawn and defined by sharp contrast to others; others with whom we in fact hold a great deal in common. Indeed, the more similar these others are to us, the more seems to be at stake in distinguishing ourselves from them (as if, deep down, we fear being absorbed into one generic, impersonal human mass, with no specific affiliations or defining features, a pulsing trans-individual blob with anonymous characteristics and no sense of identity whatsoever... a multitude without qualities... a monstrous, gestalt manifestation of what the Italian philosopher Giorgio Agamben called "whateverbeing").

The following portraits may be too general to be considered "types" in the contemporary sense, with its bias for marketable subcategories. "The parent" or "the lover" or "the poet" are descriptors capacious enough to contain any manner of gender, ethnicity, orientation, and so on. As such, there is a utopian potential in taking a fresh look at these genres of humanhood, since they can create a productive collaboration between identity markers, even between the ones that usually divide rather than connect. Very different people — with very different ethics or politics — can, for instance, bond over the trials of being a parent, or having one's heart broken by the One That Got Away. As such, these metatypes have something to say about both the specifics of their particular phenomenology and the universality of being a being among other beings (and trying to "work things out," in the most perplexing existential sense, without a shared instruction manual). Put differently: almost anyone can decide to become a surfer, provided their body is up to the task, and provided they have conquered their fear of sharks. But within the surfing community, there is represented every color, creed, age, and identity. Nevertheless, when a flotilla of surfers is waiting together for the next big wave, they are — in a profound sense — all of the same type. No matter their background, or position in life, they are watching the incoming breakers intently, paying focused attention to the timing of the elements in the hope of catching the next perfect wave. The surfer is thus a type, albeit a very elastic and contextual one. And as each surfer closes their eyes at night, they are united in replaying the soothing rhythm of the oceanic swell behind their eyelids. As a result, the surfer is a type that transcends the triviality — the obsessive identity-border policing — of so many of our seemingly infinite types and typologies. Perhaps, at the end of the day, what we do, and why we do it, is more important than who we are (or who we think we are).

The thirty examples in my own gallery of characters — found in the following pages — seek to highlight the connection points that we forget or deny even exist between very different types of human being, or simply between different ways of being human. They do this even as they also celebrate the specificity of a particular pinhole perspective on life: whether this be the perspective of their job, their fate, their curse, or their calling.

An Invitation

I invite you, dear reader, to treat the following pages as a gallery space.

In this space hang thirty portraits, sketched in my preferred charcoal of words. Each portrait depicts — in a provisional and provocative way — a different way of paying attention to the world. When taken together, as a kind of updated tarot deck, they flesh out a new adage or proverb: "You are what you pay attention to." Each type presented ahead is therefore an attempt to highlight some of the typical ways in which we have been *taught* to pay attention, often in ways that seem natural but which in fact are nothing of the kind. Certainly, you are what you pay attention to. But you are also *where* you pay attention, *how* you pay attention, *why* you pay attention, with *what*, and with *whom*. (You are also what you *don't* pay attention to, either deliberately, out of spite or aversion, or unconsciously, out of ignorance or neglect.) The broad collection of human types offered ahead represent the tension created when different ways of navigating life pull or twist in different directions (especially when highly specialized approaches come into conflict with the general, shared forms of attention that comprise "society itself" as a whole).

No doubt, the list of figures is potentially endless: proofreaders, translators, sports commentators, cool hunters, lifeguards, trainspotters, trendspotters, bird-watchers, census takers, quantity surveyors, and so on. Indeed, I do hope readers feel inspired to consider and unpack their own examples. But

I also hope the gallery of caricatures that awaits is enough to give an overall sense of the stakes involved when we opt to pay attention in a specific, culturally coded (and thus culturally *loaded*) way. Only in fully recognizing these stakes will we begin the difficult but necessary adventure of conceiving — and then *actually practicing* — ways of "attending otherwise."

The Parent

The parent — one hopes! — pays attention to her child.[1] The new parent in particular experiences a deep, bodily — even biological — imperative to pay attention. For hundreds of thousands of years, humans have been obliged to watch their offspring carefully, since the helpless, infantile stage of our species is extraordinarily prolonged and vulnerable compared

---

1 This and all following portraits are, in the first instance, thought experiments. They are also *figures* (since figures, like animals, are "good to think with"), and not descriptions of actual people. They are an amalgam of all possible instances of their type. A problem arose, however, as soon as I was obliged to insert pronouns, since it then becomes necessary to provide a gender identity for a figure that is perhaps best rendered as universal. Were the English language equipped with a long-standing gender-neutral pronoun, I would most certainly use it. The ones currently being suggested by non-binary folks (xe, ze, sie, and so on) are, however, still unfamiliar and thus distract from the grammatical flow. And so I have opted to switch between feminine and masculine pronouns, depending on the figure under discussion, each one adopted, one way or the other, for specific rhetorical, polemic, or aesthetic reasons. (After lengthy experimentation, I abandoned the idea of using "they / their," since the idiosyncratic nature of each figure has more force when presented in the singular. This also has the advantage of avoiding possible confusion when contrasting the single figure against plural instances.)

to other creatures. Too long spent cooking the mammoth steaks or painting the cave walls could mean the little one, dozing in the corner, is suddenly snatched by wolves. While many first-time parents in our own time panic at the thought of suddenly safeguarding the bare life of their new bare-bottomed baby — and procure every "How to" book they can find in preparation for this daunting task — most also talk of an instinctive care program that kicks in naturally, in response to the first cry of fear or hunger from the newborn. (The evolutionary process has ensured that the cry of a baby is, to our ears, the most alarming and demanding of all organic sounds, practically requiring urgent attention from the parent at the level of DNA.) Mothers in particular, given the profound bond created through nine months of fleshy coexistence and co-habitation, sometimes speak of a kind of invisible umbilical cord that continues to attach their life to the fresh, chaotic vitality of their child. Even as the parent works in one room, she tends to keep at least half an eye (and ear) on the child in the next. She is forever paying a kind of continuous, semi-conscious attention to the welfare and well-being of the child, and springs into action whenever the crashing and wailing begins.

This is not, however, to deny the existence of neglectful parents or deadbeat guardians who pay more attention to their own desires and vices than the needs of their children. But the role of the parent — historically most sanctified in the figure of the mother — requires a special kind of cognitive focus that toggles between the juridical ("Don't eat dirt, Sally"), the pedagogic ("What letter comes after G, Carlos?"), and the task of socialization ("What do we say when someone gives us a present, Alicia?"). The parent pays attention to a child's mood in order to ascertain the degree to which she can breathe more easily and perhaps even finally continue other tasks that need to be done. She constantly scans the child's body for any sign of harm or illness. She ensures that the child is fed at least enough to keep the poor creature alive, and is often obliged to remember dietary foibles, aversions, and allergies. She pays attention to her child's coalescing personality so that she can encourage certain traits and trajectories, while subtly — or not so subtly — discouraging others. She pays attention to her child's quirks and symptoms, hoping that the kid is not already suffering from so called attention-deficit disorder. As the young one grows, the parent pays attention to their grades, their clothes, their comportment, their attitude, their friends, and the various social ripples they create around them. She notices the way the child reflects her own character and proclivities, like a compact mirror catching the sun, distorting these in the process. She contends with the way the child is an apple, either rolling quickly away from the tree or sitting closely to the trunk, perhaps already going a bit floury in the process. (The parent is even expected to pay attention to the mood and comfort of strangers in the park or on the train, who may be disturbed by the boisterous curiosity, or simple shrieking, of the child. She is expected to simply vanish, taking the noisy brat with her.)

On top of all this, the parent is at least dimly aware that she is modeling the art of paying attention to her child, and that if she doesn't demonstrate the benefits of sustained focus, the child may forever bob between one caprice and the next, like a cheap champagne cork. A "good" parent, who pays proper attention to her child, helps them feel loved, validated, and special. We are all aware, however, of the existence of that fine line between welcome attention and suffocation or a kind of enabling spoliation — even if no one can be certain of the exact location of such a line. It is expected that a parent will pay enough attention to her child to meet their physical and emotional needs, but also leave them alone enough to cultivate their own identity and independence. Classic literature, and indeed Hollywood, is replete with examples of parents who were not able to navigate this tricky double-act. From the father of the brothers Karamazov to the Joan Crawford–style mothers who torment their young in lieu of their own demons, the parent is a highly ambivalent figure, one whose attention can begin to feel like surveillance, or even sabotage. Proust's *In Search of Lost Time*, for example, begins with the young narrator, Marcel, desperately trying to squeeze more of his mother's attention out of the rapidly waning evening before he resigns himself to sleep. She, however, is engaged in the parlor with the standard socializing of her epoch and class. This quest for a final goodnight kiss, stolen from the strangers who themselves stole his mother from his presence, feels almost as epic as an Icelandic saga, as Marcel agonizes to himself, for page upon page, about how in fact he might get the supplementary maternal attention he craves (exhibiting a sense of entitlement and urgency that will animate all the significant encounters to come in the novel). By our tween years, however, parental concern and consideration is usually enough to mortify us, as we pray our friends do not notice the maternal tissue wiping away a smudge on our cheek before school.

Freud, in turn, built his entire psychoanalytic edifice on the Oedipal attention economy, whereby the son inevitably becomes resentful of the attentions that the mother is still obliged to pay to the father, and thus wishes the latter dead. (As we shall see throughout this book, attention is almost always considered a finite resource, subject to the rules of a zero-sum game, and if someone is the beneficiary of it, someone else is not.) Fathers, for their part, often feel jealous of the newborn and begin acting out because the mother is now paying all her attention to the child. The domestic economy has shifted.

Which is all to say that a parent is destined to fail, since no one can pay the right quality and amount of attention, in the right direction, and for the right amount of time, all of the time. Even so, we set this scenario up in our subconscious minds as an ideal situation from which we all suffer, either by not providing attention or by not benefiting from it. The parent is expected, on a good day, to provide ideal attention, and yet we all know this is unrealistic and impossible, even with the best intentions and conditions (loving parents with limitless resources). As such, the structural failure, or attentional deficit, of parenthood itself haunts all our subsequent relationships and understandings of what it means to notice, acknowledge, respond to, dwell with, and so on. (On some level, we all — at least occasionally — feel like an orphan: that is to say, someone whose attentional invoice has not been paid.)

Whether we decide to have children or not, we are all shaped by our parents (or by the imagined contours of the absence of parents). "Hey, Mom, look at me!" is a demand quilted through all of our endeavors, whether we admit it or not. And to a four-year-old, a distracted parent is akin to a distracted God or Goddess. "Why did you create me," asks the four-year-old, with their sulky eyes, "if you are not going to worship me in turn? Why breathe life into this clay, if you are not going to shower me with your constant blessing, like the ever-generous sun, shining forever, in a cloudless realm?"

The Doctor

The doctor pays attention to the patient through the cultural prism of refined skills, techniques, and experience, acquired through countless generations. A doctor becomes so only after lengthy study and supervised apprenticeships working with the sick and infirmed. As such, the doctor's attention thus moves between an enduring, yet ever-evolving, body of knowledge and the entropic, ever-devolving body of the patient. It is an impersonal kind of attention, guided by clinical observation. This is not to say that the doctor cannot be emotionally involved in the welfare of her patients, or guided by compassion. But ultimately, the doctor's attention is highly focused on the symptom or disease, and dedicated to eradicating it as best she can (even to the detriment of the person afflicted, as so often happens with chemotherapy, for instance). The doctor — in the modern, so-called Western sense — pays attention to the symptoms as they present themselves to, and through, medical technologies: the stethoscope, the X-ray, the blood pressure pump, the MRI scanner, and the lab. This kind of attention isolates, highlights, and delineates.

There is more than a glimmer of the detective in the practice of medicine. The doctor pays attention to the patient's account of their own symptoms, but only as a smudged window onto the reality that the body itself ultimately lays bare in its mute honesty. The doctor must make intuitive connections, and ingenious deductions, in order to offer an accurate diagnosis.

The sick person, it must be admitted, usually has too subjective a view on their own condition, and is thus expected to defer to the doctor for a more scientific and dispassionate interpretation. (The patient tends to attach their specific suffering to larger narratives entwined with their identity, or — even worse — to rather random pages on *WebMD*.) The doctor, however, is the one in a position to compare the compromised organs, bones, tissues, and nerves with the results of recent trials, experiments, surveys, and studies.

As soon as the sick person submits to a medical examination, the patient exchanges their own intimate, idiosyncratic experience of illness for the generic charts, exotic databases, and standardized procedures of biopolitical hermeneutics (including what José van Dijk calls "the endoscopic gaze").[1] The doctor's attention is thus shaped by the prevailing professional wisdom of the epoch, forever subject to revision (itself a complex process, shaped by technological advances, government regulations, economic interests, corporate pressures, and so on). Depending on the doctor's specific location and situation, she may be obliged to take into account extraneous factors, such as the suitability or unsuitability of her own protective equipment during a pandemic, or, for example, the tactics of aggressive protestors surrounding an abortion clinic.

Many doctors feel a deep investment in their vocation and a deep dedication to their patients, to the extent that it can be a kind of spiritual calling, or at least an abstract form of prioritizing the Other. On countless occasions, a doctor will risk her own health for that of people she has not even

---

1   José van Dijck, *The Transparent Body: A Cultural Analysis of Medical Imaging* (Seattle: University of Washington Press, 2005).

met yet, let alone formed a relationship with. On the other hand, the doctor can also be a figure of neglect, indifference, distrust, menace, and even abuse (as the American Olympic gymnastics team can sadly attest). In such cases, the doctor allows himself — let's admit, *this* kind of doctor is usually a man — to pay far too much attention to his own desires, and is intoxicated by the authority that his position represents. (Compare this to the late nineteenth century, when doctors became so tired of stimulating their "hysterical" female patients to orgasm, a supposed cure for their neuroses, that they invented the vibrator so such patients could now treat themselves in the convenience and privacy of their own homes.)[2]

In any case, since the time of Hippocrates, the doctor has embodied that essential kind of attention that allows the rest of us to persist and continue as long as humanly possible. The doctor's attention intervenes at moments when our own threatens to become swallowed up by pain or pinned in place by discomfort, turning inward and becoming an obsessive, demonic version of itself (attention so focused on its own troubled consciousness that it reads to others, on the outside of personal somatic distress, as distraction). Medical attention in modern times can seem callous, as the human being who is ill can all too often be seen as *getting in the way* of their own convalescence. The sick person is too often considered an inconvenience to be endured or tolerated in the pursuit of a cure. No wonder so many people today look to "alternative medicine" when feeling unwell. They are searching for a less hyper-focused form of care, one that considers the *entire being*

---

2   Rachel Maines, *The Technology of Orgasm* (Baltimore: Johns Hopkins Press, 1998).

of the patient, including the psyche and the soul and the various networks and contexts that support them. Such people seek attention to the *holistic* self, for whom pain may originate in places beyond the anatomical location of the symptom, even beyond the physical body itself. Traditional Chinese medicine, for instance, has yielded all sorts of fascinating maps of the human body, making counter-intuitive pairings between organs, and an entire highway system of meridians connecting the complicated *polis* of the physique. Acupuncture is thus an exquisite form of reengineering, clearing blockages and creating new energetic detours in real time. Likewise, the European doctor of the Middle Ages paid attention to a patient's humors and prescribed concoctions and procedures that would help balance a body's internal climate. But even long before *The Lancet* and Harley Street, there was a strict distinction between the kind of doctor who carried leeches in his breeches and the village "healer" or untrained midwife. The former enjoyed the cloak of broad social legitimacy, even as his own application of the *pharmakon* might harm as much as heal.

In short, the doctor represents a type of attention that is both impersonal and profoundly intimate. We tend to *submit* to doctors and defer to them — sometimes even transferring onto them — due to their position in society, their almost sacred task, and their "magical" powers. Our lives can literally be in their hands, as in the surgical theater, and so we pray they have excellent attentive powers. This type of attention is thoroughly professional but also requires a delicate understanding of the personal (what we call "a good bedside manner"). It is the doctor who brings us into the world, and the doctor who confirms when we have successfully left it. And on the basis of that mortal bookending alone, she enjoys a special place in the general attention economy of our kind.

The Hypochondriac

The hypochondriac pays attention to himself as if he were an eternal patient. Indeed, he shares a great deal in common with the doctor. They are, however, polite mortal enemies. The hypochondriac is the bane of the medical expert's life, showing up at the doctor's office again and again with symptoms that are psychosomatic, at best, or completely imagined, at worst. The hypochondriac pays careful, ongoing attention to his own physiological system. As such, he is in a constant state of both shock and awe: shock that his body — a complex and exquisite symphony of metabolic processes — manages to function from one moment to the next; awe that this performance does not collapse completely given the almost infinite number of things that can go wrong.

The hypochondriac's bible is *WebMD* and Drugs.com. He is a connoisseur of painkillers, fever reducers, anti-inflammatories, as well as other, more exotic, bespoke pharmaceuticals tailored to his particular physiological idiosyncrasies (unless, that is, he is a member of the "wellness" clan, in which case he has cupboards full of vitamins, herbs, bone broth, and supplements sourced from deep in the last remaining patch of rainforest). The hypochondriac thus pays intense and focused attention to his own physical well-being and the ever-expanding universe of diets, superfoods, exercise regimes, and wellness routines that are said to maintain it. One might say that a hypochondriac pays an unhealthy amount of attention to the notion of health. And as such, he is in special thrall to what German philosopher Martin Heidegger called the *They*. (The *they* being, in this case, an anonymous kind of shifting consensus, as deployed in a statement such as, "*they* say that we should be eating more blueberries and omega fatty acids now.") He scans the world's medical news reports and fringe blogs in a bid to gain enough amateur knowledge ("They say that selenium will help fight Covid") to become his own doctor and eventually dispense with the official dispensary (and by the same token, dispense with the humiliation of being considered a nuisance, a diva, or a delusional waste of precious time).

The hypochondriac is thus an ambivalent figure who wants to be his own doctor while also deferring to the authority of actual medical experts. Moreover, he is a perverse figure, since he uses his almost monomaniacal obsession with the fragility of his own mortality in order to *escape facing that very same thing*. Rather than look into the eyes — however near or far — of the grim reaper, he parcels out his finitude into palatable bundles, rationing out biological entropy into manageable moments and units. Each symptom is thus, paradoxically, a distraction from "the End," even as the anxiety that swirls around it originates in a profound sensitivity to the same. It is a superstitious, homeopathic operation (which also explains the hypochondriac's enthusiasm for homeopathy). The final irony of all these psychosomatic stutters and contortions is that the hypochondriac dies a thousand deaths, while the courageous person dies only once (as Julius Caesar famously noted). Every minor symptom — a sore throat, a slight dizziness — is immediately followed by a pessimistic diagnosis, a worst-case scenario. The hypochondriac is thus an unqualified doctor who gleans some kind of dark pleasure from being the first to inform himself that his condition is, indeed, terminal.

(The perfect epitaph of the hypochondriac: "I told you I was sick.") And this is why the hypochondriac is such a nuisance to medical professionals: they're an unprepared understudy forever trying to usurp the starring role.

The hypochondriac is shunned in polite society because he pays more attention to his own body than to the social one. He is only interested in his own, corporeal state of the union and cannot contribute meaningfully to the greater human project. He is too distracted by the impersonal skeleton beneath his flesh just waiting to jump out at him (or rather, *from* him) as soon as he lets down his guard. If we are in a charitable mood, however, we can acknowledge that there is something impressive about the hypochondriac. There's a feat of chronic concentration, a high-wire hormonal balancing act. The hypochondriac is one of the many modes of the narcissist. (Indeed, classical sources tell us that once Narcissus cottoned on to the fact that it was *his* reflection staring back at him in the water, this comely youth used the organic mirror as a way to check whether the small bump on his lip was a cold sore or perhaps something more serious.)

During a pandemic — like the one which currently rages invisibly outside my window — the hypochondriac comes into his own. Indeed, it's strange how germophobes can, on occasion, suddenly be cured of their debilitating condition when the air is replete with plague, as if the onset of their own personal nightmare somehow frees them from the prison of their neurosis since their acute vigilance is now shared with the wider population.

Distracted by the eloquent solicitations of his own symptoms, the hypochondriac is, ultimately, an attention seeker. He seeks to be inserted into the loving bosom of the medical system, where the entire edifice of the Hippocratic art is brought to bear on his humble person and thus validates his existence (albeit precariously, and even negatively). The chart of his daily vitals, hanging on the wall by his hospital bed, speaks to him like a seismograph of his own inscrutable soul. And he feels an irrational relief when he is — finally! — officially afflicted.

The Shrink

The shrink pays attention to the mental traces and verbal webs of her patient. No doubt she is familiar with hypochondriacs, who are among the many colorful species of neurotics that grace her couch. (All humans are, by psychoanalytic definition, neurotic — just to differing degrees.) She may or may not technically be a doctor, but the shrink enjoys the same authority as that profession due to the deference we give to the authorized dispenser of diagnoses. In addition to the rather modern sheen of the psychotherapist, we still detect the strong incense of "the Viennese witchdoctor" in any therapy session, no matter how prosaic the office or how scientific the prompts (hence the term "shrink," which carries a strong racist and anthropological association with the "head shrinking" of exotic tribes once imagined to populate the "dark continent"). Freud did not help matters when he described the unconscious as "a cauldron of seething excitement." Nevertheless, it is the shrink's job to stir this cauldron and examine what strange souvenirs the ladle brings up from the soupy concoction contained in our minds.

The shrink is, above all, expected to pay attention to what the patient says. This is not, however, the standard type of listening, but rather a stereophonic variation whereby the analyst listens with one ear to what the patient *literally* says (manifest content), and to what he or she is *actually* saying, or alluding to — between the words — with the other (latent content). This is to say, a shrink must pay attention to both text and subtext simultaneously. As such, she embodies an almost sacred form of attention, one that can penetrate the shadows of appearance and see into the more enduring truths of our kind (albeit a form of truth hand-sewn to fit the plight of each individual analysand).

For the shrink, the person on the couch is a parched portion of agon, and it is up to the therapist's divining skills to find the *aqua vitae* blocked within in order to release it. The shrink must thus pay attention to the topography of their patient's psyche: the bogs, the deltas, the isthmuses, the quicksand, as well as the sloping valleys in which fresh breakthroughs may flow. Various oblique techniques have been developed to access these trapped resources and these repressed experiences and feelings. Word association, dream interpretation, hypnosis, Rorschach tests, and other "modalities" (as Lisa Kudrow's cringe-inducing "web therapist" calls them[1]) are designed to catch the unconscious "sleep talking," briefly unhindered by the wily and vigilant censors of the conscious mind. (It could be said that each patient is a four-dimensional Rorschach blot for the analyst to interpret, an analogy that recognizes a certain amount of projection on the part of the shrink herself during diagnosis and treatment.) The shrink pays attention to jokes, verbal tics, and the famous "Freudian slip," attributing deep meaning to seemingly trivial slips of the tongue. It is her calling to outwit the sophisticated defense mechanisms we have all developed in order to minimize not only ego bruises, but also super-ego sprains and id splinters.

---

1   See the innovative and underrated TV show *Web Therapy*, co-produced by Lisa Kudrow, and aired on the Showtime network, from 2011 to 2016.

The shrink is, in some respects, an accountant, making an audit of the psychic cost of sublimating our animal instincts and creaturely freedoms. She is attuned to the cost of stepping into the restrictive straightjacket of human intercourse, even as this process comes with certain social benefits. One of her most effective techniques is to pay attention to what we ourselves pay most attention to: whether these be transitional objects ("Where is my blankie!"), libidinal investments ("Go local sports team!"), erotic fetishes ("May I caress your shoe?"), misrecognized targets of resentment ("Immigrants are taking our jobs!"), or other decoys of disavowal, our own psycho-attentional economy is a revealing map — through its negative space and unclaimed places — to what we are *really* interested in (that is to say, to what we are *really* interested in *avoiding* thinking about or confronting).

According to the shrink, the objects of our attention are almost always alibis for our *not* facing up to the original trauma of becoming a person (one now responsible for our own thoughts, feelings, desires, and comportment). For Freud, we are forever haunted by the authority of the father and our guilt for wishing to either castrate him or finish him off altogether (or both). We are also forever entangled in the taboo of incestuous feelings for our first love — the mother. The energy required to repress such emotional swirlings can lead to perversion, hysteria, and even psychosis if not acknowledged in homeopathic doses and sublimated into compensatory cultural activity. For Lacan — who dusted the Victorian furnishings of Freud's theoretical edifice so that more modern folk may inhabit it without allergic reaction — we are forever attempting to fill an existential lack at the heart of our being: a lack we attempt to banish by singing ourselves lullabies of personal completion, and by "finding our better half." Even more tellingly, Lacan believed we are forever watching ourselves through the eyes of an imagined Big Other, whether this be the patriarch, the master, the leader, the boss, the cop, the examiner, the judge, the teacher, the priest, or even God himself. Such a scenario has enormous implications for the shrink, who must now figure out which Big Other is the "structuring absence" in the patient's account of their own biography. Who, while explicitly ignoring them, is the patient really paying the greatest attention to? Whose blessing are they seeking without even realizing it? Who is the invisible audience for their painfully self-conscious performance of their own identity? And which key people, gathered along the way, have been enlisted to play unwitting roles in the ceaseless Oedipal drama of their lives?

No question then, shrinks have a daunting job, and they are not immune from becoming the surrogate Big Other of the patient through the famous process of transference. All too often, those unacknowledged and unresolved feelings are projected onto her as a convenient figure of what Lacan calls "the One Who Knows" (a process explored with vivid intensity in *The Sopranos*). Transference is thus a workplace hazard for the shrink, and she must protect herself by erecting clear personal boundaries like a verbal electric fence. She must constantly pay attention to whether the patient is paying *too much* attention to *her* — trying to divine her approval, her boredom, her disgust, her cloaked feelings being scribbled on a notepad — rather than to the matter at hand. And so the shrink must constantly steer the conversation back to the narrator-protagonist of the session, lest the patient dump the gelatinous contents of their own seething cauldron right over her head.

No doubt, we all find ourselves in the position of the shrink from time to time, whether we are qualified or not. A conversation between friends can quickly become a free counseling session as we deploy our various patchy understandings of pop psychology, assembled from talk shows and half-remembered text books. "The talking cure" is indeed often conducted for free, over phone lines or in coffee shops, and without warning, to the extent that many of us feel we're actually participating in "emotional labor" as much as good old-fashioned friendship. Conversely, we may feel entitled to inflict our amateur diagnoses on friends and family — even to stage an intervention on occasion. The professional shrink, by contrast, can be an object of distrust, or even fear, for friends or relations of the patient. They may consider her to be an expensive crutch, or an enabler of further narcissism (though Adam Phillips makes a compelling case for the Freudian wing of the profession when he writes that psychoanalysis "frees people to lose interest in themselves; [since] there's nothing more self-preoccupying than a symptom, nothing finally less interesting than one's self").[2]

All of which is to say, when it comes to attention, the shrink is expected to weave together scientific expertise, ancient wisdom, good instincts, professional objectivity, impersonal sympathy, paranormal sensitivity, anti-counter-transferential vigilance, and many other things besides. She is a figure that inhabits many worlds at once, unsettling us, in her anachronistic persistence through epochs, but also seducing us with her silent promise to decode the enigma of our own, personal, preposterous existence. In the perverse pretzel logic of her kind, the more we pay someone else a fee to pay attention to the *way* we pay attention to ourselves, the more chance we have to be eventually freed of the overwhelming burden to do so.

---

2   Adam Phillips, *Attention Seeking* (London: Penguin, 2019), p. 26.

The Detective

The detective pays attention to signs or clues. As such, his vocation — as with the doctor and shrink — is primarily a semiotic endeavor. He must pay careful attention to details that others have missed or discounted as irrelevant. Usually, the detective's task is to discover the identity of the murderer, at least in his literary or screen incarnation. (In real life, a detective is probably more concerned with rather banal, albeit consequential, transgressions such as money laundering or insurance fraud.) In any case, this archetypal figure is traditionally credited with being an eagle-eyed member of the attention economy: someone who knows not just *how* to look, but *when*, *where*, *why*, and for *what*.

Whether your favorite example of the profession is Sherlock Holmes, Philip Marlowe, Miss Marple, Nancy Drew, Inspector Morse, Kojak, Poirot, or Columbo, each detective has a different comportment — a different style-as-stratagem — that she or he brings to the job. The detective often attempts to outwit the guilty party into incriminating themselves. They may thus seduce, trick, fool, cajole — or even sometimes simply *annoy* — the truth into revealing itself. This can take many forms, from disingenuous confusion (Columbo), to shifty street-smarts (Sam Spade), to collective persistence (the gang from *Scooby-Doo*). No matter the technique, the detective tends to have figured out who the culprit is long before a confession is forced from them.

Some critics have argued that the detective novel is the purest of all the fictional genres, providing a meta-commentary on the process of reading itself. From this perspective, the detective adopts the role of a narrator, disguised as a character, who intrudes into the narrative itself in order to help further and explain the logic of the story. In this case, the sequence of events exhausts itself in the congealed clot of fully thickened plot. (Detective stories are often described as "page-turners," in the sense that each revelation or twist happens in a linear manner, like the falling of dominos. This is also, however, the reason why detective novels are seldom read twice, since once the mystery is solved, the story vanishes in its own resolution.) At any rate, detective stories are pleasurable to the extent that the reader, or viewer, is obliged to shadow the detective, usually piecing together the puzzle in tandem with the highly attuned sleuth, and in a convincing simulation of real time. (It is rare that the reader or audience is given more evidence than the character tasked with figuring out the mystery in the story.) As such, the reader or viewer is in cahoots with the detective, and thus in a slippery relationship with the *author* (who may or may not reveal the truth at any given moment). Hence the authorial deployment of decoys, feints, red herrings, loose ends, shaggy-dog stories, false twists, and so on, since the trail of clues must be part breadcrumb, part pebble in order to keep the interest of anyone following along (both inside and outside the world of the story). The detective is thus a mirror image of the author: a storyteller in reverse and in retrospect.

The detective works with tracks, traces, prints, residues, shadows, and the general material wake of human ships, passing through the night. His famous process of *deduction* relies on contingent elements that only later prove to be decisive: the placement of objects, the quality of light, the muffled nature of a sound, a lingering scent, and so on, all filtered through the five senses and then synthesized through a sixth (specifically, the enhanced intuition that is essential to the job — something which places the detective rather close on the attentional spectrum to the shrink or fortune-teller.) As such, he is also concerned with "structuring absences" and the negative silhouette of the guilty party, traced by the environment itself (a sharp contrast to the police chalk that bluntly delineates the victim and his or her previous life). In addition to this kind of inverse police sketch — identification by proxy — the detective is obliged to attend carefully to the elusive qualities of mnemonic recall, as filtered through the fragile and faulty faculties of the witness. Which memories are false, partial, imagined, or otherwise compromised? This is the question that the gumshoe is forever wrestling with and must pay extra attention to.

Today, the detective relies on various prosaic computer skills, looking for digital traces online via cookies, IP addresses, MAC addresses, and other electronic indicators. But in the golden age of private detection, he was exquisitely attuned to the *indexical* nature of the crime: the singular way in which the guilty hand scribbled her signature in ink (not to mention the chemical signature of the scent, cleverly used to cover the smell of gunpowder). In the golden age — from the Victorian era, through the noir-esque decades of the 1930s and '40s, up to the invention of the Internet — the profession relied on hyper-focused attention to material traces: cigarette ash, lipstick, scuff marks, bullet holes, stray fibers, lost buttons, misplaced furniture, and so on. The detective was an expert reader of faces as much as of rooms. And unlike the forensic professional, who would in many ways supersede him, the detective of bygone times was concerned with mood, gesture, and other intangibles (that is to say, with the virtually undetectable transgressions and repressions that inevitably prick their way into consciousness by the final act).

This is why there is something anachronistic about the more modern detective, who relies on a resolutely analogue or organic skill set, in contrast to the criminal investigator, whose brain is merely a glorified messenger between the crime scene, the morgue, and the lab. Whether portrayed as a fool (Inspector Clouseau) or as a hirsute alpha male (Magnum PI) — or some other twist on the classical formula established by Arthur Conan Doyle — the detective is a rather belated figure, one who stubbornly insists on *noticing* things when the rest of us have blithely, and even happily, outsourced our senses and attentional faculties to machines. Were he to finally renounce his ineffable gift for reverse engineering criminal enigmas, the detective would become merely a technician, swabbing for DNA or brushing for fingerprints. In that case, he would be about as ingenious as a smoke detector, trained to recognize only a limited set of patterns or elements out of an infinite series of possible combinations. (And perhaps it's worth noting in passing that this is partly why detectives will always be higher up on the totem pole than detectorists, the latter relying on machines — namely metal detectors — to unearth Roman coins, Rolex wristwatches, and other ancient treasures and modern oddities from the soil or sand.)

In short, the detective is a romantic and nostalgic figure who represents the kind of heightened attention that we can no longer bring to bear on even the famous cinematic representations of his kind. He is an emissary from a less distracted age, when we were still capable of "taking stock" of the world. As such, he embodies our collective wish for a stubborn human capacity to outwit even the clinical genius of DNA tests and motion-detecting surveillance cameras. The detective recognizes not only that the devil is in the details, but that the detail has its own diabolical habit of exposing its own sin (and implicating the guilty party in the process). Whether smoking a pipe or sucking on a lollipop, the detective finds perfect coherence in the random nature of the universe. And as such, he is something of a reverse Tasmanian Devil, leaving order in his wake, wherever his own personal whirlwind takes him.

The Lover

The lover pays attention to the beloved. At the same time, he pays attention to the rituals of love itself. Indeed, in many ways the lover pays attention with more intensity than any other figure we can care to name. Especially in the first throes of his amorous affliction (since this portrait will focus on *romantic* love), the lover is passionately concentrated on the beloved to such a degree that all other members of the community fade into the background, back into a gray and indistinct generic human murmur. He is a monomaniac, concerned only with the object of his adoration: everything the beloved one says, does, and feels (whether this be in the past, present, or future). Moreover, the lover is a semiotic glutton, forever looking for signs of recognition and reciprocation. From a certain philosophical — and even biological — perspective, the lover is a *diminished being*, since his attentional aperture suddenly becomes localized, compromised, and narrow, matching the precise, idiosyncratic contours of his obsession's silhouette. The lover can thus be compared to the tick, which waits dormant in a tree, activated into life only by a certain chemical trigger. Indeed, from the point of view of the dispassionate, he appears to have the agency of a mousetrap. (George Bernard Shaw famously quipped that a lover is someone who exaggerates the difference between one person and another.)

The lover is thus a quizzical creature, at once enhanced and contracted, dispersed and focused, hyperactive and strangely passive (depending on the criteria brought to bear). Indeed, his is a paradoxical case, incandescently alive and pathetically blinkered. Nevertheless, there is something perversely expansive about the lover's specific phenomenology, since even the most arbitrary object, sound, or scent can plunge him back into the infinite sea of his amorous feelings. Every scene and situation, no matter how forsaken, potentially becomes an intimate index of secret blisses — even a discarded piece of litter reminding him of a seemingly innocuous prop in a thrilling sentimental adventure. In this fashion, the entire world becomes an oyster in which his beloved sits enthroned like a rare pearl.

To those obliged to be in the frenzied orbit of the lover, his disposition often appears as an acute case of distraction rather than attention. His knee jiggles up and down. He unthinkingly tears a paper napkin into shreds. He does not listen to the conversation, except for possible cues to talk about his affair. Is this attention or its inverse? To anyone but the beloved, it is surely the latter: a case of impatience to find himself once more in the company of the only person who *matters*. For the object of affection, however, the lover's attention can often be felt as a burden, or even as a kind of laser-guided assault. If the intensity of feeling is not reciprocated, the lover becomes a tiresome incarnation of Pepé Le Pew, who seizes his erotic quarry with clumsy arms and unswerving persistence at every opportunity.

For the psychoanalyst, love is usually a case of mistaken identity or misrecognition (just as it is with Pepé Le Pew, who mistakes a cat for a fellow skunk). According to this view, the lover trades the familiar features of an original fixation for reasonable facsimiles of the same, reincarnated in another. (In the famous case of Lolita, for instance, a wandering mole that jumps from one young girl to another, across the decades, becomes Humbert Humbert's alibi to initiate a largely theatrical endeavor in which the lover performs his own passion, in a hyperbolic mode, mostly for his own sake, and where the catalyst of infatuation is largely a physiological fluke.) Freud may insist that the person we love as an adult is but a fleshy reprise of our parental archetypes, but in doing so he misses the many ways in which the heart is a cunning and creative organ, forging *new* opportunities for desire out of an ever-expanding cast of characters. If pressed, however, we may concede to the psychoanalytic belief that love's pleasures can be difficult to distinguish from the smile and sigh of a contented baby. Certainly for Freud, love is but a musky echo of the warm, milky satisfaction of infancy and a necessarily doomed attempt to re-enter the Oedipal Eden from which we've all been banished. Such an interpretation, however, does not account for the ways in which the lover will strategically *delay* consummation or gratification in a bid to dwell as lingeringly as possible within the suspended intensity of pre-*jouissance*.

Indeed, one way to keep the intensity going — albeit in a negative way — is to see the world through green-tinted glasses. Here, the lover dons the deerstalker in a bid to play the detective. Lipstick traces on a collar, a blonde hair in the shower, a false note buried deep within a laugh — even a stifled yawn — can be considered clear evidence of unreciprocated passions, and worse, sensual betrayal. No form of attention is more sustained, and more exhaustive, than that of the jealous lover, for it attempts to vindicate his own insecurity: "Aha! I knew it. There is no way you could love me, and only me! And now I have *proof*." Of course, such attention has the unfortunate effect of alienating the beloved, who may well be innocent of the grotesque crimes being ceaselessly committed in the suspicious lover's mind. Jealousy is all too often a self-fulfilling prophecy. (The attentional apparatus of the *ex*-lover is also worth considering, as a retrospective machine that pays special mind to various fractured lenses and other devices of disenchantment. As Swann admits in a daze after his passion for Odette unravels: "She wasn't even my type!") In the beginning of a passionate love affair, attention is luminous and exhilarating. No one pays as much attention to anyone or anything as a lover pays to their beloved. Ironic, then, that they miss so much.

At any rate, if the student listened to the lectures of their professor with the same rapt regard as the lover — or if the king listened to the laments of his subjects with the same sensitivity — then the world would be a much rosier place. As it is (and as we have already noted), the lover is both a paragon of attention and its antithesis. Some will go so far as to condemn romantic love as unethical in its propensity to raise one person up above the multitude, thus casting every member of the latter into the abyss (especially if it will help the couple safeguard some quiet time together). The lover is self-involved, even as his every thought spools out toward the Other. His heart completes a closed and covetous circuit, beating a telegraphic tattoo back and forth. And it is the task of religion and ethics to open this circuit up so that the lover may share his tender compassion more widely, and more equitably (hence the important, but impossible, demand: "Love thy neighbor").

One difficult thing about the lover's discourse is that it forever seeks a signature or seal of authenticity where no one has the authority to make such a determination. Nevertheless, we feel as if we *know* it when seized by the real thing. Love can thus be a type of revelation or epiphany, an awakening *to* a form of attention as yet unknown. To his friends, the lover may appear to be a willing victim of hypnosis. From the perspective of the latter, however, the others seem to be a gathering of so many somnambulists, sleepwalking through life. In any case, the literary consensus on love, when not dwelling on its tragic trajectory, is to at least begrudgingly celebrate the way that it catapults us into experience itself, beyond the rather instinctual habits of the naïf. According to this line of reasoning, love is the pole we use to vault out of our animal darkness, over our fragile and fleeting humanity, and into the angelic luminosity of eternity. Here, love is a paradigmatic event, allowing the blood to pump as if for the first time and the scales to fall from one's eyes. Thanks to the fresh poison of Cupid's arrow, the world transcends mere mundane facticity and becomes something far more rich, coherent, and present, in all those vague yet compelling Germanic ways italicized from Goethe to Heidegger. Love is thus felt as a spiritual awakening, and the beloved plays the role of muse, guide, and medium through which the world is re-presented as potentially infinite. (This is why love is so often associated with beauty as "the promise of happiness" — though we could easily reverse those terms.)

For the lover, the beloved is a fate or destiny — an assumption that becomes awkward once he is obliged to make the same declaration to a different visage. The lover's body thus quivers with the tension created by trying to hold the unique and precious singularity of the beloved in one hand, and the imminent exchangeability of the same in the other. Excepting those rare cases of lifelong monogamy, the lover (who is, by nature, portrayed as a serial thriller) must learn to make the same promise to different paramours. And no matter how sincere in the moment, the fact remains that a lover loves a unique variation on a generic theme (an insult to the sense of specialness that love can so intoxicatingly provide us with, but also a deeper philosophical lesson in our own anagrammatic nature). The lover thus pays a kind of stereoscopic attention to the beloved, seeing both what is unique about that person and what is shared with others. (Your conviction that your lover has the best ass in the world, for instance, can only be based on an understanding and appreciation of other asses.) The beloved is thus metonymic of the human race as a whole, and stands for "that oceanic feeling" which old fusty Freud claimed to never make an acquaintance. Love is thus an apprenticeship in the profoundly vertiginous experience of what Leo Bersani calls "impersonal intimacy": the hard-won wisdom that every caress, and every kiss, is as unique as a snowflake, even as it is the snowstorm that envelops us.

The lover, on some unconscious level, knows that the beloved could have been — indeed, still could be — someone else. This simple, rather distasteful fact haunts the romantic couple. And yet it is also the condition of its existence, and thus something to be celebrated if viewed from the right, ultimately philosophical angle. Alain Badiou, for instance, believes love to be "the extended victory" of "chance defeated." It is thus "a declaration of eternity to be fulfilled or unfurled as best it can be within time: eternity descending into time."[1] Love is, therefore, the ongoing alchemy of turning contingency into destiny, not out of simple-minded, stubborn self-mythologizing, but out of a clear-eyed reckoning of the ways in which both modes inform each other, through retrospective storytelling as much as through wordless gestures of adoration.

The false lover secretly condemns the object for not being a passive, flat screen on which to project his specific desires and inclinations. The true lover, however, is especially enamored by the knots and "crooked timber" of this particular emissary of humanity. Moreover, when not merely engaging in dual-narcissism — or "autism for two"[2] — the lover loves what the

---

1   Alain Badiou, *In Praise of Love* (London: Serpent's Tail, 2012).

2   The Invisible Committee, *The Coming Insurrection* (Los Angeles: Semiotext(e), 2009).

other is striving to become, and loves them even more for failing to achieve it.

For many, love is merely another word for genuine attention and should be cultivated, matured, nuanced, and shared as widely as possible. But for others, it is a pathological symptom of our incapacity to pay attention in any kind of considered, deliberate, democratic way. In either case, the lover is meta-attentive, paying special attention to the attentions that he receives (usually measured against those given to others). His sensitivity is exemplary, but also leads to all kinds of blind spots, misreadings, and complications. Whether the lover is paying attention to the world or retreating from it very much depends on the erotic protagonists comprising the terms of the relationship. And it is between the public sphere and the private that the lovers — ideally symmetrical, reciprocal, distinct, and entangled — forge new methods and languages for paying attention, and also for paying homage.

Homage to what, exactly? Every lover may have a different answer to this. But in general, love is a name we give to the materialized impossibility that the here-and-now not only really exists, but can be *shared* — be witnessed from two different angles — rather than simply endured. The lovers (now speaking in the plural), instinctively understand that the metallic tang of time can be beaten into gold leaf, hammered into joyful shapes, and hung from the earlobe as much as from the loop of the moon. Lovers create quantum cocoons within the Newtonian fabric of the wider world. And as such, love itself is a miracle of human engineering.

Love is, after all, something we make.

The Fan

The fan pays attention to the object of her adoration. As the name implies, the fan is a fanatic. While the meaning has been diluted in recent years to describe almost anyone with even a passing interest in something specific, the fan, in its truer sense, is a proudly obsessive follower of a specific figure, group, genre, or other miscellaneous category. Whether it be baseball, K-pop, or science fiction, the fan is monomaniacal about her loyalty to, and deep understanding of, her chosen passion (hence the accusation that a fan is "one-eyed" in her unwillingness to entertain the perspective of fans of a different stripe).

While enthusiasm for specific talents or public figures is presumably as old as human society itself, fandom is a modern phenomenon, emerging from the increasing democratization of the arts and the subsequent rise of what some rather sneeringly call "the culture industry." Nineteenth-century actors and singers such as Sarah Bernhardt, Enrico Caruso, and Jenny Lind garnered passionate fans around the world thanks to the increased speed of international travel and the fledgling technology of recorded sound. More than a century before the infamous melee between the mods and the rockers on Brighton Beach, there was the Astor Place Riot of 1849, in which nearly thirty New Yorkers lost their lives. This was a pitched battle between two mobs: one, ardent fans of the American actor Edwin Forrest, and the other, equally committed devotees of the English thespian William Charles Macready — both insisting that *their* man was the superior incarnation of the spirit of the Bard. Across the Atlantic, more than a century before Beatlemania and Elvis hysteria seized an entire generation, "Lisztmania" — a term coined by the poet Heinrich Heine to describe the indecorous enthusiasm that always accompanied the handsome Hungarian's piano recitals — was sweeping Berlin and Paris.

The fan pays attention to her object of fascination in more expert and nuanced ways than the casual dabbler. She forms or joins a community to refine her knowledge and expertise. Driven by libidinal force — either explicitly or unconsciously — the fan has fully cathected onto the object of her desire (cathexis being an almost mystical projection of selfhood toward and *into* another). To be a fan is thus to be in love, with all the ambiguities and ambivalences of that highly charged state of being. The difference, in this case, is the impossibility of reciprocation. The fan will never find her passion reflected back to her by her idol (except on vanishingly rare occasions, which do not tend to go well). Yet the fan is content to dwell in this state of unacknowledged adoration, since there is something about the asymmetry of the situation that underlies the fan's pleasure or satisfaction.

The fan assembles her identity around the object of her fandom in the same way an artist slaps wet newspaper onto a wire frame in order to make papier-mâché. She finds her true purpose in recognizing the genius or allure of the Other, and feels that her own humble existence is somehow animated, and even validated, by the power of this recognition. (She is the one who *knows*.) The fans' attention, considered collectively, is crucial to the aura or mystique of a celebrity. (Imagine a rock star playing to an empty stadium. Suddenly their status as "star" is rescinded, as many a "washout" or "has-been" can attest.) But the attention of any one given fan is negligible, at best. So the fan, in the singular, is somewhat parasitic on the object of her obsession. Yet that same object is dependent on her (when scaled up to the plural), and thus always afraid that they may be "canceled" due to a public mistake or simply in the passage of time and due to the inevitable waning of interest from the fickle public. (Every public figure must fear, at some level, that they are an emperor wearing no clothes, and live in subsequent dread of a disillusioned fan pointing this out to the others in a convincing and consequential way.)

In the case of something like sports, fans tend to indulge in what Freud called "the narcissism of minor differences." Somehow, the antagonistic tribalism of the Yankees vs. the Red Sox trumps the fact that both tribes love the same game (and as a consequence, a Yankees fan hates a Red Sox fan, and vice versa, much more than he would hate, for instance, a soccer fan, despite sharing the same passion). Moreover, fandom tends to be coded as lower class, or at least unsophisticated, perhaps a legacy of Kant's argument that the true subject of aesthetic experience should be "disinterested" — this is to say, impartial. This is no doubt why we have divided up different types of enthusiasm according to a hierarchy of their embodying subjects: the aficionado, the buff, the enthusiast, the connoisseur, and so on. The fan sits near the bottom of this pyramid — the only step lower is the groupie — even though we could have, as a culture, decided to extend the same common term to those obsessed with cigars, opera, wine, and high-end hi-fi equipment.

Roger Ebert created a notorious diatribe against fans when he wrote the following:

A lot of fans are basically fans of fandom itself. It's all about them. They have mastered the Star Wars or Star Trek universes or whatever, but their objects of veneration are useful mainly as a backdrop to their own devotion. Anyone who would camp out in a tent on the sidewalk for weeks in order to be first in line for a movie is more into camping on the sidewalk than movies. Extreme fandom may serve as a security blanket for the socially inept, who use its extreme structure as a substitute for social skills. If you are Luke Skywalker and she is Princess Leia, you already know what to say to each other, which is so much safer than having to ad lib it. Your fannish obsession is your beard. If you know absolutely all the trivia about your cubbyhole of pop culture, it saves you from having to know anything about anything else. That's why it's excruciatingly boring to talk to such people: They're always asking you questions they know the answer to.[1]

No doubt, if Ebert were still alive today, he would despair at the way the Internet has spawned so many more ways to be a fan. Networked popular culture generates ever-mushrooming franchises and standardized aesthetic niches. More recently, Jarrett Kobek has voiced his contempt for fans who limit their creative expression to dressing up as focus-grouped avatars . "In the liminal zone of the comic book convention," he writes, "trapped within the magick circle of *cosplay*, it will be impossible to determine whether this 45-year-old man has any conception that he is not, in actuality, the intellectual property of a major corporation."[2]

---

1   Roger Ebert, "The Fandom Menace," February 4, 2009. https://www.rogerebert.com/reviews/fanboys-2009

2   Jarrett Kobek, *I Hate the Internet* (We Heard You Like Books, 2016), p. 148.

Fans straddle the line between passionate and obsessive, which is why they can become stalkers or worse. Steven King's bestseller *Misery* is a harrowing tale of a fan who kidnaps a popular writer (no doubt a version of the author himself) in order to ensure the swift production of another book. In comparison, consider the real-life case of Mark Chapman, who became one of the most hated people on the planet when he expressed his admiration for John Lennon in the form of four bullets. (The figure of the fan thus embodies the conflicted feelings inherent in the Oedipal scenario, eventually leading to the punk phrase, "Kill your idols.") Fans are both solicited and feared by celebrities as well as by the stewards of certain industries, since both need fans to retain their status. Fans, however, also threaten to turn on them.

A fan is committed to overlooking, or at least forgiving, the flaws of the object of their passion. As such, there is more than an element of Stockholm syndrome involved. Indeed, there is often something compulsive about being a fan, to the extent that, over time, she begins to resent her passion ("I hate my interests!" declares Steve Buscemi's character in *Ghostworld*). After a while, it can feel like an obligation, set to autopilot. While being a fan suggests a certain level of deference or subservience to the object, or at least a structural asymmetry, this can sometimes flip such that the fan feels like *they* are the one empowered to "own" the source of their original interest. Returning to the example of Star Wars, the fan of this franchise tends to pay more attention to the source material than the people who made the films in the first place. They pore over the narrative, frame by frame, with the hermeneutic intensity of a twelfth-century theologian. Except, on this occasion, while the films themselves retain biblical status, it is the *fans* who decide what is heretical and what is not when it comes to canon law (to the extent that fans feel emboldened to re-edit the films for purity, rearranging the sequence of events — "Han Solo did not shoot first!" — or even removing characters altogether, as in the case of Jar Jar Binks).[3] Fans today feel like they have ownership over their beloved objects by virtue of the quality and duration of their attention. This is no longer a passive kind of devotion — in which creativity is limited to arranging an altar to a favorite musician or sports star — but an increasingly active endeavor. Fan art and fan fiction have sanctioned the devotee to tailor the original object of inspiration into a more personalized vision of whatever captured her attention in the first place. The relationship between creator and audience is thus blurred, as fans can find themselves garnering fans themselves thanks to their idiosyncratic reappropriation of their own fandom. (The global publishing sensation *50 Shades of Grey*, for instance, began life as humble Twilight fan fiction.)

In the attention economy of the twenty-first century, the fan is at once the driving force of cultural consumption and also one of its most conspicuous producers (especially at the level of online "content"). One wonders, however, in a world of so many micro-aesthetic possibilities, whether the "die-hard fan" has in fact already died and now merely haunts these breezy dilettantes, who switch their interests and allegiances with the ease and speed of a TikTok video.

---

3   For more on this phenomenon, see Alexandre O. Philippe's 2010 film *The People vs. George Lucas.*

The Gourmand

The gourmand pays attention to the sensual pleasures associated with his appetite. Since he is usually untroubled by any concerns about where his next meal is coming from, and takes its punctual arrival for granted, the gourmand (aka the "gastronome") is less concerned with sustenance than *delectation*. Indeed, a "healthy appetite" is more than just a precondition for being a gourmand: it is both origin and destination, source and fate. In other words, the gourmand chases the impossible dream of both satisfying *and* prolonging his hunger, since this contradictory condition would allow him to simply continue eating with no end in sight. The gourmand thus dreams of being seated near Zeno's paradoxical kitchen, sampling delicacy after delicacy, but never reaching the end of the meal (a dream explicitly acknowledged by the mantra of French waiters when serving up the next course: "*Bon continuation*").

Certainly, the gourmand loves nothing more than patting his swelling belly with satisfaction after finishing a good meal, then loosening his belt a couple of notches, along with his spirit. But just as *post coitum omne animalium triste est* ("every animal is sad after sex"), every gourmand attempts to fight off a nagging melancholy that inevitably arrives with the mints, coffee, dessert wine, and bill of fare. His taste buds may have been ravished, but his culinary libido has also been reduced to ashes. And so he totters home and waits for his appetite — his constant companion, his own personal raison d'être — to return.

The gourmand can be divided into two essential types: active and passive. The latter tends to be a regular fixture at their favorite restaurants, eateries, and food stalls, chewing, gulping, nibbling, and slurping all the sweet and savory delights on offer (the lucky ones even get paid for indulging in their passion, as food critics). The more active type tends to become either an accomplished home cook or even a serious chef, turning his calling, and his refined palate, into a business. Of course, many gourmands switch between these two modes (as we saw with Anthony Bourdain, who began his professional life as a cook but later "came out" as a passive, albeit very busy and conscientious, "foodie").

Perhaps we are being too hasty, however, in describing the gourmand and the "foodie" in the same breath. After all, the latter has only really emerged as a cultural type in the last few decades, whereas the gourmand has been a fixture in the social and cultural landscape for hundreds of years (the apex being the Frenchman Jean Anthelme Brillat-Savarin, author of what many still consider the culinary Bible, *The Physiology of Taste*, published in 1825). We tend to picture the gourmand reclining on his chaise longue and snacking on a chicken leg between meals, or even eating a full meal lying down on his stomach in imitation of the ancient Greeks. As befits his passion, the gourmand tends to be unapologetically voluminous, wearing past meals on his thighs, hips, buttocks, and chest like fleshy medals of honor. Indeed, he may proudly trace his ancestry back to the Romans, who even built a special room — the notorious *vomitorium* — in which to heave out semi-digested delicacies in order to make room for more.[1] The foodie, by contrast, tends to be more disciplined in his approach to eating, enjoying the meal but being sure to match his caloric intake with time on the treadmill. The foodie may even turn his love of food into a "passion project," keeping track of new restaurants and new buzzworthy chefs via an elaborate system of spreadsheets, apps, and Pinterest pages. This is to say, the foodie is what remains when the gourmand is stripped of his bourgeois infrastructure, and thus his unimpeachable alibi, for succumbing to the cardinal sin of gluttony. Moreover, the foodie is what happens when the bon vivant is suddenly forced to contend with the competitive and judgmental mediascape of contemporary life.

The gourmand still evokes the excessive days of Rabelais such that the act of eating can quickly turn into something more sacrificial — a potlatch of his own appetite (as explored with such grotesque humor in Marco Ferreri's surreal 1973 film *La Grande Bouffe*, in which a group of four friends decide to eat themselves to death in a vague yet visceral protest against the modern world). The gourmand's propensity to excess, however, should not be confused with an "eating disorder," since that would be to approach the phenomenon through the lens of pathologized, individualized psychology, rather than the generic and ceremonial symbolism that he truly merits. Through the act of excessive ingestion, the gourmand —

---

1   Recall the grotesque figure of Mr. Creosote, from Monty Python's 1983 film *The Meaning of Life*, who — after a truly gargantuan feast in his favorite fancy restaurant — is tempted by the waiter into eating one single "wafer thin mint" before exploding over the entire room.

like the characters in Ferreri's film — protests modern (or even more enduring Protestant) values such as moderation, temperance, self-discipline, frugality, and so on. With every bite, and each accompanying moan of delight, he exults in a saturnine desire to gorge on the entire world, a world now compressed into one single morsel. All his sensual attentions are thus focused intently on the enduring infantile desire *to ingest* the world[2] (and from this point of view, the gourmand is also sublimating his latent cannibalistic instincts).

The foodie, for his part, is not so primal or allegorical, since he takes pleasure from food in a more circumspect and "ethical" way. For while he moves in a similar attention ecology to the gourmand — noting and appreciating all the elements that "frame" the meal, such as the ambiance of the room, the service provided, the tableware, the menu, and so on — he is more sensitive to questions of provenance, treatment, sourcing, distribution, carbon footprint, and so forth. The foodie attends to the political economy designed around his appetite, and attempts to meet it at least half way. The gourmand, usually a man of independent means, is not so obliged to take his pleasures with a pinch of salt. The foodie,

---

2   Freud famously notes that for the infant, sexual pleasure and the satisfaction of the appetite are found in the same object — the mother's breast. This is why we instinctively understand the intimate proximity, even confusion, between food and sex. From this perspective, we may assume the gourmand is sublimating his sexual desires through the consumption of food. But we may just as well reverse the scenario and explain the sexual compulsive as rechanneling his unresolved feelings regarding the act of eating into the relatively straightforward mechanics of copulation.

however, is compelled to function within the social and economic pressures of the modern world. He must hustle and instrumentalize his connoisseurship and expertise. In other words, the foodie is expected to contextualize, communicate, and *perform* his pleasures. (A gourmand, for instance, would never even think to take a photo of his meal and put it on Instagram.) If the gourmand is involved in an old-school love affair, wooing his food like a culinary Casanova, then the foodie is an efficient and amiable, but ultimately too self-conscious and distracted, friend with benefits.

Yet I'm being too hasty again in painting the gourmand as a caricature of old-world affluence, since this level of passionate connoisseurship can be found at every level of society, provided the appetite in question can retain its original integrity. (Take, for example, the gruff truck driver in Juzo Itami's wonderful 1995 film *Tampopo*, who understands the almost infinite nuances involved in making a good bowl of ramen; or the group of nomadic homeless men in the same movie, who ramble around Japan breaking into restaurant kitchens overnight to whip up quick meals worthy of at least one Michelin star.) When it comes to the question of attention, the gourmand is ultimately a problematic figure, since he is, by virtue of being enthralled by the drama or romance unfolding on his taste buds, trapped within his own narcissistic — even solipsistic — adventure. On the other hand, we can only assume he also appreciates the old adage that a pleasure shared is a pleasure doubled, and would not object to a pleasant dining companion (provided he or she was similarly dedicated to the delights of the table). The foodie may be more social, but only in the preoccupied mode of "social" media. He is still too worried about whether the parsley is sticking in his teeth, or whether his latest blog post has garnered enough views, to truly savor that last oyster.

At any rate, both inflections of the same obsession speak to the fact that we are, as a society — and even a species — rapidly losing both the art of eating and the art of eating *together*. More often than not we eat at our desk, or on our sofa, or even standing at a counter, too distracted by whatever we're watching, or obsessing over, to even taste the food (which, again, more often than not is unworthy of really being tasted). Even in France, the spiritual home of the gourmand, strident moves are afoot to banish the traditional two-hour midday meal in an effort to synchronize with the more business-friendly schedules of the EU. *Commensalism*, the bonding act of sharing a table, is an increasingly endangered experience in the age of bankrupted restaurants, drive-through takeouts, and four-device family dinners. (Were Jesus condemned to death in the year of our Lord, 2021, he might find it a challenge to convince twelve of his disciples to even attend the Last Supper.)

Which is all to say, the gourmand — and his more ubiquitous cousin, the foodie — practices a kind of unconscious resistance to the reduction of life to bread alone (gluten-free, no doubt) or to the start-up staple of Soylent (a tasteless gray supplement conveniently designed to replace actual food with a daily dose of vitamins, minerals, and a deep gnawing sense of meaninglessness). The gourmand provides some grounds for hope in his unashamed attention to the needs and desires of the body in a world committed to telling the body what to do, how to do it, when, and what to look like while doing so. In a culture dedicated to shaping, measuring, weighing, and disciplining the body, the gourmand is a scandalous and inspiring figure. He listens to the wishes of his *entire being*, understanding that the soul is not only found in some abstract private chamber of the heart but also in the generous and friendly mess hall of the stomach. Despite his many flaws and foibles, then, the gourmand — in his wise, unproductive use of time, his generous and voluptuous embrace of consumption that transcends mere consumerism — can help us to grope our way back to a more nourishing and delectable mode of being, and especially of being together.

The Student

The student pays attention to everything except her studies. Or so it seems to her professor. Indeed, one wonders if the Platonic ideal of a student ever existed, even at Plato's academy, two and a half thousand years ago. Today, she is seemingly intrigued by anything and everything, with the exception of her assigned reading or the droning lecture of her educational shepherds.

Her mind wanders. Her pen doodles. She is thinking of something that just happened or may happen later. The student feels attached to her studies in the same way that a prisoner in a chain gang is attached to his ball of iron. With the invention of the smartphone, the student experiences class or homework as nothing other than a Promethean ordeal to be suffered as inconspicuously as possible. Of course, the teacher is a practiced observer and recognizes the signs of mental drift in his charges with the laser-like acuity of a hawk recognizing a rodent shifting about in the autumn leaves. And while the teacher may dream of a class filled with wide eyes and hungry minds gulping down his hard-earned wisdom without any form of distraction, he is obliged to be content with the increasingly rare overachiever, whose attention somehow feels like a burdensome compensation for the lack of interest displayed by the overwhelming majority of the group.

The student is not only studying her chosen subject (or the subject foisted upon her), but *learning to learn*. She must internalize the discipline that her teacher claims to have already mastered by the time he was the student's age in order to perhaps eventually reach the same place — playing the role of expert and social super-ego all at once. As such, the student is an apprentice broker in the attention economy. Before she crosses that magical membrane separating the undergraduate from the graduate, however, the student is a puppy or a kitten, let loose in a giant library but only interested in the tassels hanging off the furniture or the cords that lead from lamp to socket. Parents, despairing at their offspring's grades, turn not only to tutors, but to doctors, who pronounce the dreaded diagnosis: attention-deficit disorder. Expensive drugs are prescribed, designed to harness a wandering mind and eventually propel it, like Zeus's chariot, toward the solar warmth of concentrated focus. As such, the student is one of the most visible symptoms of the accelerating attentional entropy that teachers lament even as they themselves drift from their lesson plans, fondling their phone in the vain hope of a sudden offer that might free them from the role of glorified babysitter.

One wonders, however, if the drastic reduction in the student's attention span has been exaggerated precisely to sell more such pills. After all, who has the experience or authority to judge what constitutes a "deficit" in the first place? (And does this relocation of the term suggest that some people have a "surplus" of attention, as may happen with some fixations that occur "on the spectrum"?)

Long before the invention of solicitous pocket-technologies, Friedrich Nietzsche wrote:

> The student listens to lectures.... Very often the student writes at the same time he listens to lectures. These are the moments when he dangles from the umbilical cord of the university. The teacher...is cut off by a monumental divide from the consciousness of his

students.... A speaking mouth and many, many ears, with half as many writing hands: that is the external apparatus of the academy; set in motion, that is the educational machinery of the university.[1]

This is to say, Nietzsche understood that attention was a rather modern commodity that needed a whole machinic assemblage in order to produce it. But produce it from *what*, we may ask? *Ex nihilo*, in fact. Or from the *tabula rasa*. From the unrefined clay of the student's mind.

As education lurches online, a kind of willed and mutual attention — the kind found, miraculously, in seminar rooms even today — becomes increasingly difficult to encourage and sustain. The student feels her presence to be a simulated effect of shadowy, faceless companies running vast banks of machines. She therefore finds it almost impossible to cathect onto her own intellectual potential. Her head is less in the clouds and more in "the cloud" (which, as the critics like to remind us, is just someone else's computer). To an increasing degree, education is obliged to exercise its tired muscles in the two-dimensional nowhere space of proprietary software, which cannot incorporate the body proper. And while we may think that the absence of the body, with all its fleshy distractions, could help with the goal of focusing the mind, it turns out that the organic actuality of the individual is essential to the underlying Eros of education.

Eros in what sense? Well, the student will only submit to the rigors of intellectual instruction if she falls in love with the *idea* of knowledge (itself the promised road to wisdom). In this

---

1   Quoted in Friedrich Kittler's *Discourse Networks 1800/1900* (Palo Alto: Stanford University Press, 1992), p. 18.

sense, philosophy is indeed the paradigmatic form: the love of knowledge or knowing. Before anything, the student pays attention to her teacher with a kind of merciless precision and X-ray vision. (Any doubts about this will be dispelled with a quick visit to RateMyProfessors.com.) The student notices how her instructor looks, speaks, stands, and smells. She notices his tics, his gestures, his expressions, his moods, and his various props and talismans — a can of Diet Coke, an old watch removed from the wrist and placed on the table, three different colored whiteboard markers (arranged on the desk in a specific order to superstitiously enhance the chances of surviving another day after facing the open-mouthed aquarium of his underinformed charges). Such attention is the basis of a special bond which, over time, transmutes into a kind of faith, or at least trust. "Yes teacher," the student seems to be saying. "I recognize your foibles and your failings. I see your disappointments and vexations. But I also acknowledge you know more than I, at least about this topic for which we have gathered. And so I shall instruct my brain to manufacture some glutinous attention, like the sap of a young sapling, through which you can hopefully help make some useful, edifying information stick." Together, the student and the teacher form an attentional loop. And while this loop is vulnerable to breaking down, it is also blessed with the potential to create new forms of intellectual wattage — fantastic new types and shapes of lightbulb — suspended in the crackling air.

Learning today is a heroic endeavor, especially given the fact that the student's attention is being deliberately assaulted from all angles, twenty-four hours a day, by diabolical genies of weaponized distraction. There is a war on for possession of the minds of a generation. And the first task of the teacher is to alert the young that they are conscripts already in the midst of a battle they cannot yet understand, or even really see.

The Voyeur

The voyeur pays attention to the object of intimate, oblivious exposure. Somewhat akin to the lover, the voyeur is seized — at one and the same time — by kaleidoscopic distraction and laser-focused attention. Distraction arrives in the form of all those specific colors, shapes, lines, tones and textures that the voyeur craves and seeks out, like a bloodhound, but that refuse to stay still or be pinned to the mat by his lewd gaze. These formal properties — made flesh and framed by windows, clothing, and other contingent furnishings and accessories — may indeed be simply squandering their radiant bounty elsewhere, without so much as an erotically excitable witness, like a sun that shines on a long-abandoned planet. And this undeniable fact drives the voyeur to the brink of madness. For if he could, the voyeur would sublime himself into the sky and become a sun of sorts, an all-seeing eye — a human panopticon — that is able to spy on every single private moment of interest, to probe himself into each and every intimate disrobing, each unseen vignette of wasted *frisson*.[1] Instead, such figures — and such moments — almost always spill themselves into the gutters of unwitnessed happenstance, like a mid-priced bottle of champagne knocked over by the belligerent elbow of a drunken regional manager, the shapely vessel glugging itself empty of any further squandered intoxications. This is to say, the erotic tableau of the bathing woman, or the risqué vignette

---

1   Cf. the hit single "Eye in the Sky," by The Alan Parsons Project (1982).

of the consorting couple, usually happens — merely *occurs* — without the hot "stamp" of the voyeur's gaze.

The voyeur is driven to distraction by all those precious scenes that remain not only unphotographed, but completely unseen. The very idea of a woman, draped in wispy undergarments, yet uncaptured by paintbrush, or those little pixelated prisons we carry in our pockets, provokes him to chew on the corners of his moustache in frustration. (This is why the voyeur is so often seen carrying a camera, or, as in the case of at least one man in Japan, affixing small mirrors to the tops of his shoes, to enable peeking up the skirts of unwitting commuters.) The end result of such libidinal distraction is that when the voyeur *does* manage to engineer, or simply stumble upon, some kind of scopic access to a potentially titillating display, his attention suddenly becomes hyper-focused. For the voyeur, his person of interest is as well-defined as one of the animated silhouettes in the enchanting film-fables of Lotte Reiniger. She both emerges from her mise-en-scène, like Aphrodite from the foaming waves, and then detaches herself as pure foreground. (There is no depth of field when it comes to the mental cinematography of the voyeur.)

We see the essential architecture of voyeurism in Alfred Hitchcock's *Rear Window*: the seer and the seen, connected by an invisible thread of intense observation. James Stewart's character, rendered immobile and at the mercy of his neighbors for entertainment, begins as a "disinterested" witness (in the Kantian sense), but becomes more interested in the comings and goings of his fellow citizens as a suspicious series of narrative possibilities emerges from the life-sized dollhouse across the courtyard. While Stewart's glance may flirt with following the nimble movements of the ballerina across the way, these are not his focus, and thus we may ultimately consider him more of a witness than voyeur. (Though we may note in passing that Hitchcock's entire filmography has been described, by some critics at least, as little more than an overly polished archive of one embittered man's voyeuristic obsessions, specifically with blonde bombshells possessing a masochistic streak.)

We may be quick to condemn the voyeur for his sadistic scopophilia, as well as for his weakness in allowing the infamous male gaze to infect and define him,[2] but this would be to disavow the voyeur inside all of us — the roaming drone of our desire to see that to which we do not normally have access. This, of course, explains why television is so popular — and films before that (and painting before that), since visual representation is a technology that stores voyeurism for later, and for our own convenience. Technology time-shifts the curious gaze, and in doing so normalizes it. We are all Peeping Toms, Tinas, and Taylors.

The *locus classicus* of the voyeur is just outside a bedroom window. He peeks in, perhaps himself hidden in accommodatingly placed bushes. The main tool of his trade is a pair of binoculars. Like a young seamstress lusting after an expensive dress in a department store window, the voyeur indulges in *lèche-vitrine*, or "window-licking." Desire is expressed and further encouraged through frustrated ingestion. Indeed, the pane of glass somehow enhances the enchantment as both barrier and portal — a banal manifestation of X-ray vision. The voyeur is on the hunt for public breaches in private moments (as when curtains accidentally part on an intimate domestic scene), or, alternatively, private moments in public spaces (as when a couple furtively caress, mistaken in

---

2   See Michael Powell's controversial 1960 film *Peeping Tom*.

the belief they are unheeded). The attention economy of the voyeur rises and falls according to the enigmatic gestures of affection: for another human being, for oneself, for a pet, for the gentle reciprocity of surfaces, for an unthinking routine, swaddled in fatigue. As such, the other most likely place to find a voyeur is peering through a keyhole, as in the penny arcade favorite *What the Butler Saw* (itself a clever meta-commentary on the desire to see, and indeed to pay a pretty penny for it). Here a lady on vacation, or at least at leisure, succumbs to the cajoling of her mischievous companion and stoops to look through the viewfinder. There she spies on a situation in the midst of a budding mise en abyme: her suitor watches her blush, as she watches the maid blush at the behest of the butler who noticed the scandal in the first place. The invention of the camera enshrined the human genius for turning our proclivities — some may even say our vices — into objective technical functions or capacities, outsourcing voyeurism to a more magnified and mobile medium.

Today, an entire scopic economy is built around the ubiquity of phone cameras and webcams, crystallized in the popularity of digital platforms like TikTok and OnlyFans (the latter simply an X-rated version of the former). And in sharp contrast to the past, young women today consciously curate themselves as the objects of voyeuristic desire, referring to themselves as "thirst traps."[3] The prey of such sensual snares is no longer known as a "voyeur" — which lends a certain kind of old-world Gallic dignity to the affliction — but rather a "simp" (which at least has the virtue of introducing a linguistic

---

3   Where the old adage used to say, "Dance like no one is watching," young TikTokkers today dance like they hope the algorithm will notice.

asymmetry of power into the situation to the advantage of the historical victim, aka, the person being seen).[4] Moreover, what is the much-maligned "selfie" if not a mirrored portrait of auto-voyeurism, the frozen document of the schizoid attempt to inhabit the space of both desirer and desired in a strange loop of foreclosed digital prurience.

When the invisible talons of Covid sent us all scampering inside, we were obliged to become voyeurs to a compounded degree, since even the relatively innocent hobby of "people watching" was banned in real life. Those who lived in condensed areas could reenact *Rear Window* if they chose, but were more likely to do so by watching reality TV on Netflix. For those more enamored of Mother Nature than her nubile daughters, a new collective passion for bird-watching was discovered, as this was a pastime that could be conducted in the relative safety of the open air, and involves no victims (unless we consider the desire to watch birds bathing in the morning sun a special kink in its own right).

When all is said and done, the voyeur's specific form of attention will never be truly satisfied, not in the long run, since he searches for something he cannot ever *really* see. Any given thirst trap only serves to make his thirst stronger, for even if she disrobes completely, he will see only anatomy, physiology, flesh. But the voyeuristic eye craves a connection to something more metaphysical. As Roland Barthes notes, when it comes to

---

4   Today, the biggest voyeur of all is Silicon Valley: Facebook, Google, and all the other leering companies that secretly stuff cookies in our pockets so as to better follow our every click and comment, our every post and communication. They salivate in anticipation of the metadata that we shed like dried skin, forming the Chladni figures of our online portraits.

"the end of the striptease," the point is "no longer to drag into the light a hidden depth, but to signify, through the shedding of an incongruous and artificial clothing, nakedness as a natural vesture of woman, which amounts in the end to regaining a perfectly chaste state of the flesh."[5] In other words, voyeurism is based on a contradiction: "Woman is desexualized at the very moment when she is stripped naked."

The voyeur ultimately wants to visually eavesdrop on Being: that is to say, on the secret moments and activities of the Big Other. However, the Big Other does not exist. There are in fact only a multitude of little others, all trying to get by. We all feel and fear that we missed the all-important, transcendental memo that everyone else received and is diligently incorporating into their hearts, minds, and works. The voyeur in fact masochistically seeks confirmation of being left out, excluded, abandoned to his own ignorant devices. He seeks proof of his own irrelevance and insignificance. And while he finds such evidence in spades, it is not the kind admissible in a court of the realm, merely in his own suspicions. The voyeur seeks the outlines of an omnipotence and ease that will forever elude him, as well as for the source of his own tale of bewilderment, perplexity, and woe. As such, the eye of the voyeur follows an asymptotic line that may indeed faithfully trace many callipygian contours, but which will never cross the threshold of a true carnal knowledge.

---

5   Roland Barthes, *Mythologies* (London: Vintage, 1993), pp. 84–85. See also Giorgio Agamben, *Nudities* (Palo Alto: Stanford University Press, 2010).

The Journalist

The journalist pays attention to "all the news that's fit to print." She chronicles the world's affairs — both local and global — for the immediate and ongoing edification of the informed citizen, and as such, embodies the celebrated "fourth estate" of a healthy democracy. The journalist must select, from an almost infinite array of possibilities, what deserves to be the focus of her readers' collective attention (begging the highly sensitive question of whether journalists are merely reporting the news as it happens, or if they are in fact curating, even *shaping*, the news). In setting the agenda for public debate, the journalist also creates the conditions for general amnesia regarding certain experiences and stories, since not every issue or event can be included in the daily, or even monthly, bulletin (though some are passed over in silence for more complicated reasons than merely a lack of time or space).

The journalist shares a great deal with the detective, sleuthing her way to the truth, using her gut and her gumption to guide her. Moreover, she has a nose for knowing when something doesn't smell right, and has been trained like a sniffer dog to detect when an informant or public figure is trying to sell her a sizable quantity of horse feces. The journalist pays attention to things that dubious characters hope no one will notice: travel itineraries, phone records, digital receipts, administrative emails, the hasty sell-off of shares, and so on. In today's political climate, which has created a greenhouse effect for toxic authoritarian regimes, she risks not just her livelihood, but sometimes even her life in attempting to document current events on the ground and give airtime to unofficial talking points.

For some (including the historian and the philosopher), the journalist is so caught up in the tailwind of events as they happen that she can't see the deeper and wider patterns of which her dispatches are but a tiny detail. She is blinded by her own immersion in the here and now. And like a moth, she reports on a single inch of a massive Persian carpet, sometimes even mistaking crumbs for key motifs. It should go without saying, however, that both the historian and philosopher are dependent on journalists of days gone by for providing the raw material of their research and further ponderings. Nevertheless, for this same, often elitist demographic, her contributions to society are much like the cheap printer's ink that sticks to the fingers: smudged and superficial. This is presumably why Nietzsche called her kind "papery ephemerids" (and also why one acerbic character, in the classic 1954 film *Sabrina*, suggests that all journalists be beaten into the very same pulp used to make the paper on which their impertinent musings are printed in the first place). From a more charitable perspective, however, the journalist is the watchdog of the people, conscience of the republic, and guardian of free speech. She keeps politicians honest (or at least sweating under the obligation to *appear* honest), the police diligent (same caveat), and the titans of the business world on their gilded toes.

Such is the *principle* of the vocation, at least. In practice, the journalist has become, on the whole, much too cozy and complicit with the various regimes — political, cultural, economic, aesthetic — that comprise the chimeric and threadbare costume of the Zeitgeist. For every Woodward and

Bernstein — the two quintessential reporters who famously broke the original Watergate scandal — there are now thousands of lesser figures attempting to elbow into the game, often by affixing the suffix "-gate" to every minor infraction they can find or fabricate. Indeed, the entire mediascape has changed dramatically since the 1970s. And beyond the venerable BBC — where a foreign correspondent still somehow manages to correspond to traditional journalistic codes and infrastructure — the news today arrives by viral video, social media post, or half-verified rumor. Indeed, given the ascendance of tabloid journalism over the previously esteemed broadsheets — and the subsequent scramble by the latter to start imitating the former to chase the advertising dollar[1] — the journalist has become a figure who works primarily to *manufacture* scandals, and then to remind us to *pretend* to be shocked. In truth, however, we have become immune to the outrages perpetuated in public life. And yet we still click on the link for the cheap chemical squirt it may induce in the jaded and gummed up wrinkles of our gray matter.

But can we really blame the journalist for adapting to the clickbait economy when we consider the precarity she is now asked to endure? Where once the journalist sailed like a vetted member of the Royal Navy — in a large and powerful armada of banner headlines, broadsheet newspapers, broadcast radio stations, and well-funded apprenticeships — the industry has been reduced to shattered and sodden timber by the

---

1   While it is a faux pas to mention this in polite company, we all understand implicitly that the once-esteemed "gray lady" has fallen on hard times and is now obliged to totter down to the docks at 4:00 am to hitch up her faded skirts for the price of a few quick and anonymous column inches.

undiscerning cannons of popular discourse. For while it seems counter-intuitive that the journalist would become an endangered species in an age of exponential hunger for "content," she finds herself rudely replaced by bloggers, amateurs, YouTubers, home commentators, bots, large language models, and voracious cut-and-paste algorithms. No question, the general public still craves news and expert opinion. But these can be simulated — or better yet, parodied — for a fraction of the price it costs to maintain a well-trained newshound.

People still want topical information, but they want it bite-sized and easily digestible. Long-form journalism — patiently presenting several different sides of an issue, and meticulously detailing the context — may as well be a library copy of *Finnegans Wake* to those who prefer to get up to speed via the latest tweets and memes. The journalist (that is to say, the *adequately paid* journalist, as opposed to the ambitious young freelancer) is thus forced to fight for survival in an attention economy that caters to the insatiable distraction of human squirrels. No wonder we find ourselves nostalgic for the mid-century Hollywood portrait of newspaper life, in which a smart and sassy "lady reporter" has time to make a quip in between looming deadlines, exposing the framing of an innocent man for murder, and conducting a screwball romance, all at the same time.[2] Somehow even the speed of the old-school, cigar-chomping newsroom still allowed attention to detail and a focus on what "the story" itself required or demanded in a way that no longer holds today.

Indeed, one of the biggest stories of the new millennium is the speed with which such a vital organ of democracy

---

2   *His Girl Friday* (Howard Hawks, 1940).

has been ravaged by the cancer of digital "disruption." The journalist of any remaining integrity must compete for attention with influencers, industry shills, pundits, conspiracy theorists, and sock puppets. Moreover, she must find an objective perspective — or at least a rational compass — in a discourse that has been warped entirely out of shape by the nihilistic disinformation factories deliberately manufacturing reckless quantities of "fake news." Perhaps a resurrection of the profession awaits, after the whole echo chamber collapses in on itself — a phoenix rising from the ashes of some former semblance of social coherence. In the meantime, however, and in the space of only a few decades, we can only watch on in mute dismay as the epic ambition of *Citizen Kane* crumbles into the tenacious narcissism of citizen journalism.

The Philosopher

The philosopher pays attention to everything under the sun. Or rather, he pays attention to *any given thing* under the sun. Or, better yet, he pays attention to *that which offers itself up to being attended to*... under the sun. In doing so, he transmutes the prosaic texture of everyday experience (what one famous thinker called "being") into a profound secular revelation (what the same thinker called "Being").[1] The philosopher is thus something of an alchemist, forging truth out of the base elements of our quotidian lot.

In the so-called Western tradition, the first philosopher to become a household name was Socrates. This charismatic, archetypal sage wandered around Athens, inflaming the minds (and in some cases, the loins) of his fellow cogitators. Socrates was especially adept at what we today call "mansplaining": bending the ear of anyone in the vicinity, with the confidence that comes with being born on the more enfranchised side of the gender divide. (Women, lest we forget, were not deemed free citizens in ancient Greece, perhaps partly due to the lack of a beard to stroke in full phallic contemplation.) Socrates was, however, careful to deploy various rhetorical decoys around the perimeter of his intellectual convictions, usually in the

---

1 Martin Heidegger, *Being and Time*, translated by Joan Stambaugh (Albany, NY: SUNY Press, 1996). First published in German as *Sein und Zeit*, in 1927.

form of a steady series of leading questions (a now standard pedagogic technique known as "the Socratic method").

Socrates was, at the end of the day, a first-rate *noticer*. He noticed things about Hellenic society and, by a series of nimble logical extensions, humanity in general — since philosophers are nothing if not first-rate extrapolating generalists. He noticed the dangers of parochial chauvinism (as witnessed in the ongoing rivalry between Athens and Sparta). He noticed the way we tend to glom on to the virtues of individuals rather than thinking more expansively about shared, general human qualities. And he noticed the extent to which professed codes of ethics can conveniently be suspended in the pursuit of influence and riches. (Just to name a few.)

Socrates did not hoard his epiphanies but shared the gift of coherent reasoning with folk who crossed his path, seeking to sharpen the next generation's powers of perception and thus elevate the general tone of reflection and insight. Socrates indulged in this noble pastime until the leaders of the city lost patience and obliged him to gulp down a hemlock cocktail (early evidence that there are few sharper thorns in the side of power than the encouragement of awkward questions). Socrates learned a bitter final lesson, one presumes, as the toxin took hold of his nervous system: namely, that one should not pay *too* much attention to the ways of the world (and if one cannot help doing so, then one shouldn't go around inflating the local attention economy lest it overheat and crash).

Socrates' most diligent student, Plato, paid special attention to the lessons of his cherished teacher, memorializing them in the form of dialogues that even today provide the daily nutrients of a healthy philosophical diet. In these works, Plato uses his master's literary likeness to ventriloquize his own suspicion that no matter how closely we pay heed to something in, or of, this world, we are still missing something essential. Plato thus believed that any object (or subject) we encounter is but an earthly shadow of its perfect, immaterial, transcendental form. In other words, Plato was the first and foremost expert on *distraction*. In his famous allegory of the cave, for instance, a mysterious community of people sit chained in the darkness, mesmerized by flickering shadows on the fire-illuminated walls.[2] Only when these underground dwellers — these "strange prisoners" — are "dragged into the light" do they realize that they have been living all their lives inside a false reality. (It is often noted that Plato deserves a belated co-writing credit for *The Matrix*.) Soon enough, however, the people inhabiting this fable — pained by the relentless glare of truth — scamper back into their dim domestic burrow, preferring to pay attention to familiar shadows than to the harsh light of reality. The moral of the story? That people cannot be *forced* to pay attention to the True, the Right, the Good. Indeed, it is an uphill battle to convince our fellows to spend their precious attentive faculties on anything other than frivolous puppet shows made of smoke and trivial fancies.

For the philosopher, the supreme object of attention is both alpha and omega of any given mental activity whatsoever: the self. For intelligence to occur, it must be housed in and powered by a *mind* of some description. And a mind is ultimately an organic machine for processing the random appearances of existence and sorting them into legible, modular units of understanding. (Descartes could have saved precious time by simply reversing his famous adage: *I am, therefore I think*.) Philosophy — at least in its dominant interpretation — is thus

---

2   Allan Bloom, Book VII of *The Republic of Plato* (New York: Basic Books, 2016).

the journey the mind takes when rigorously tracing a long, self-regarding arc that eventually bends over into a perfect ouroboros: *know thyself*. And yet, this mental expedition — this auto-ethical imperative — is not necessarily a narcissistic detour away from "the real world," since the philosopher also understands that we can, as humans, only have a pinhole perspective on the universe. We peek out at the Infinite from the modest, mortal sunroofs of the rented terrestrial vehicles of our bodies. And thus, the more our self-knowledge is free of delusion or confusion, the more we have a clear view of the cosmos. Philosophy can thereby serve the same function as that simple but rather mesmerizing rubber tool found languishing in dirty buckets at the gas station with which we wipe the car windshield free of bugs and dust).

The same thinker alluded to elliptically at the beginning of this piece, Martin Heidegger, believed that the modern world was founded on a simple, but astonishing, act of amnesia: specifically, "the forgetting of Being."[3] For while we may *think* we are thinking, we are in fact spending enormous amounts of mental energy spinning our wheels precisely in order to *avoid* thinking. Better to stuff one's ears with the soft wadding of career, fashion, gossip, credit scores, and conspicuous consumption than listen to the Siren song of existence (which, if faced properly, arrives unmediated and in full, resplendent

---

3   While Heidegger was one of the most influential philosophers of the twentieth century, his legacy has been tarnished by his complicated, though certainly culpable, relationship with the Nazis. For more details on this sorry relationship, see *Reading Heidegger's Black Notebooks 1931–1941*, edited by Ingo Farin and Jeff Malpas (Cambridge, MA: MIT Press, 2016).

actuality).[4] Heidegger made many lyrical gestures to what he called the Open: an abstract place where humans can ascend, if and when the scales fall from their eyes. As the only animal with the *potential* to shake free of instinctual shackles, humans — according to Heidegger — are the only creatures on Earth with the capacity to make *new* worlds, beyond the organically encoded instructions of Mother Nature.[5] And we can only do this through our as-yet-untapped capacity for *attunement* (a term that essentially describes paying attention to an awesome degree). Such new worlds are not, however, the utopias promised by Silicon Valley, which in practice only serve to further trap us inside flashing glass bubbles. Instead, they are (and gird your loins for some chewy Bavarian black-bread descriptions) "in the mode of the oblivion of being, a proper mode of the truth of beings, a mode that all the more testifies to the essential occurrence of being, i.e., to the disconcealment of the open."[6]

The looping language that flowed from Heidegger's pen attempted to banish our rote and habitual attention to the

---

4   Here we can see the long shadow of influence that Plato and his cave still cast over even the most meticulous and anti-allegorical of minds. Indeed, it seems reality is never *real enough* for the philosopher.

5   Many people have pushed back on Heidegger's complicated, explicitly disavowed humanism and his recasting of the Great Chain of Being in more modern terms. See, for instance, Gerard Kuperus, "Heidegger and Animality" in *Phenomenology and the Non-Human Animal*, edited by Christian Lotz and Corinne Painter (Dordrecht: Kluwer/Springer, 2007).

6   Martin Heidegger, *The Event* (Bloomington and Indianapolis: Indiana University Press, 2013), pp.10–11.

mere surface of things — our banal autopilot registration of a prosaic world. Instead, he attempted to clear a mental space in which we could collectively attempt to remember, or reinvent, our primary encounter with existence, to re-adjust our full cognition to the dazzling miracle of the fact that "there is Something, rather than Nothing." The true philosopher, in this tradition, following in the feverish footsteps of Nietzsche, rejects cheap distraction as well as excessive attention to petty grievances. And he does so in the interest of an *authentic* (and yes, often elitist) sharing and shaping of Experience. Such a rare feat, the philosopher insists, will be accomplished through a purified process of paying attention, one that helps us learn how to *use* language rather than simply be *used* by it. This unblinkered orientation, moreover, understands something as vital as the work of art to be less an expression of vain genius than the spool upon which the heavens are threaded closer to the Earth. (And as this vague description suggests, *describing* "the problem of Being" is far easier than engineering a practical solution or path forward.)

Contemporary philosophers, influenced by this legacy, are nevertheless not so ambitious or optimistic about this potential for species-wide self-actualization lying dormant in the human condition. Nor are they so romantic as to consider these rather vague poetic gestures as the desirable endgame. Indeed, they are rather inclined to emphasize the opposite: that we are in fact trapped in a neo-Platonic loop, increasingly captivated by our own concepts and the claustrophobic machines which grow from the contaminated seeds of such. It is indeed a historical irony that the more pessimistic the philosopher becomes — the more he decries the fallen state of our age — the easier it becomes for the state to ignore him (otherwise Chomsky or Agamben would have already been slipped the hemlock milkshake by now). Indeed, philosophers are no longer condemned to death for the simple reason that no one is listening to them in the first place. They fall somewhere between drunk, avuncular mall Santas and eccentric Sunday school teachers.[7]

Traditionally, the philosophical promise is to rise above the mere technical disciplines as "the queen of the sciences" — authorized to speak of anything and everything and yet be held to no particular standards of specialized knowledge. Indeed, the proper object of contemplation is no longer restricted to metaphysics or "first principles," but includes politics, communication, and the organization of society. Nothing is deemed too frivolous to preclude the possibility of deeper instruction. The philosopher is thus obliged to pay attention to everything from the climate crisis, to shifting gender norms, to emerging digital trends (though he tends to do so at such an abstract level that he is really only paying attention to what other philosophers might say about this or that, without engaging with the problem in the material mode that it demands. This is to say, philosophers primarily pay attention to *philosophy*). Were Socrates alive today, we might see him staggering from agora to symposium, eyes spinning like pinwheels, his toga creased and smeared with grease, overwhelmed by all the stimuli competing for attention, analysis, interpretation, and explanation. Instead, we have

---

7   Perhaps this is why so many so-called moral philosophers spend much of their time coming up with "thought-experiments" like the Trolley Problem or the Drowning Child Problem, in which innocent people are forever in peril, trapped in the sadistic scenarios dreamed up by impotent, resentful, and washed-up philosophy professors.

only "public intellectuals" who make millions of dollars by writing airport books containing such rare pearls of wisdom as "If you practice something a lot, you are likely to improve," or "There exists a point at which a certain tendency is likely to topple into a different state."

Over the course of the twentieth century, and extending into this one, our professional overthinker fractured into two types: the "analytic" and the "continental" philosopher. The former tends to be logical, positivistic, systematic, and pedantic, while the latter is more poetic, oblique, abstruse, and speculative. The analytic type remains true to "the love of wisdom," but mistakes the latter for a rusty obstacle course of rather arbitrary postulates. The latter has touching faith in the real-world effects of intense thought, while doing everything possible in terms of personal expression to avoid being understood. Wisdom, for the continental philosopher, is a naïve dream at best, though it's more likely to be a dangerous delusion. For the analytical philosopher, wisdom is still within reach, if only the correct formula is devised. Even after several thousand years of humans wooing wisdom with their would-be wise words, there is little evidence of wisdom loving them back.

At the end of the day, both types of philosopher are irredeemably academic, and thus fail to speak to a broader public, preferring instead the introverted pleasures of glass bead games. They themselves pay more attention to passive-aggressive footnotes in the latest book by their professional nemesis than to the urgent, unprecedented questions of the age. But despite their own failings and mental flailings, the Ghosts of Philosophers Past occasionally return from the Other Realm to watch the living and shake their heads. As we hustle here and there, they take pity, and attempt to take us by the elbow in the town square, as Socrates once did. Then, over the din of our daily lives, they try to remind us that we are not paying attention to those three questions that matter most: *What do I know? What should I do? And what am I allowed to hope?*

The Poet

The poet pays attention to the verso of life's routine recto. As such, her verses are designed to bring out the world's more latent, under-observed qualities. This is evidently a tautological process, since anything the poet commits to the page is, by virtue of this lyrical decision, necessarily poetic. From Dante's mythic probes, to Keats' rapturous projections, to Emily Dickinson's deep and quiet yearning, to Philip Larkin's frank insistence that "they fuck you up, your mum and dad," the poet is a typographic prism, refracting the prosaic light of daily life into a shifting kaleidoscope of moods, scenes, and moments. We certainly commit an act of violence, or at least an act of supreme laziness, when squeezing all poets in the same categorical boat, for they embody so many different voices and perspectives. Indeed, there are as many ways of rendering the world on to the page as there are individual poets — the only tissue connecting their sensitive souls being a commitment to using language as economically as possible. Some poets seek to boil life down into a resinated, resonating soup stock, while others let their subject sublimate and evaporate into an elegiac ether. Some unstitch tightly wound moments, while others seek to thread together seemingly disconnected places and occasions. Beyond their idiosyncrasies, however, the poet understands that their art speaks either elliptically about direct matters or directly about elliptical things.

One exception to this rule is the haiku: a pure and distilled description seeking to capture and convey the fleeting essence of a moment in time (a moment never to be repeated, except within the poem itself). The master of haiku is a magician, pulling the *non* out from under the non-event like a tablecloth, leaving the setting undisturbed. Despite its direct gaze and unadorned expression, haiku can, paradoxically, be considered the crystallization of the poetic instinct. For the poet understands that attention is more than simply noticing things. The person who mindfully attends to the world is co-*creating* that world from one moment to the next. This is why poetry is an especially powerful practice, and why it has been increasingly marginalized by our hyper-prosaic era. (Everything is allowed to be "poetic" today, with the exception of poetry itself.) Today, the poet is suffered or politely tolerated in equal measure by the technocrats of the world-soul: persons who have been trained to see only the positive, functional, *actual* components of life and not the vast reservoirs of the unspoken, the unrecognized, the emergent, the vestigial, the anachronistic, the marginal, the clandestine, the stubborn, the confounding, the communal, the improvised, the untimely, the uncanny, the unexpected, the unplanned, the quiet, the slow, the seductive, the opaque, the unproductive, and the unprofitable.

Once again: attention *generates* reality, and *poetic* attention generates a more vibrant and capacious reality. Life is poetic, though we have to look deeper to see it. Hannah Arendt famously discussed "the banality of evil," which is certainly a ubiquitous force to be reckoned with. But what about the good of banality? This is the raw medium of the contemporary bard, and the poet has an ear exquisitely attuned to the sound of invisible trees falling in distant forests. This is to say, the world needs a *witness* in order to happen, in order to bring itself into being. (This is why solitary confinement is the ultimate punishment. If you cannot see yourself reflected in the eyes of others, you begin to wonder if you really exist.) The poet is the singular witness: a kind of idiosyncratic recording angel, transcribing events — real or imagined, recalled or anticipated — into a language forged through intimacy. In contrast to the professor, pundit, or politician — who speaks in a common, vulgar, universal tongue — the poet forges her own eccentric vernacular. One must meet her more than halfway, on the threshold of her own linguistic abode. As a consequence, the poet writes her own humble community into being, a community connected through the proximity necessary in order to peer through her unique window on the world (a window made of a pane of glass forged through elemental confusion, just as glass itself is produced when lightning strikes sand).

The modern poet tends to think in terms of frozen moments and tableaux, creating an emotionally potent mental photograph in words. The prose writer, by contrast, is involved in making moving pictures, with their own forward momentum. The poet obliges the reader to slow down, to pause, to allow their attention to roam around the snapshot which waits patiently for its secrets to be revealed. The novelist, however, beckons the reader ahead, like a prancing pied piper, catching their interest in the slipstream of plot. The first reading of a poem is usually a warm up to stretch the attentional muscles. The words lie inert on the page, awaiting the right frame of mind to activate and animate them. Only in almost liturgical repetition does the meaning of the poem — or its enigmatic force — emerge. The poet thus provides an important reminder of the superficial dangers of first impressions and taking things quickly, at face value.

Like a photograph, a good poem includes a "punctum": a small detail which "pricks" or "wounds" the reader in a sudden, unexpected, and moving way. It is just such a detail — often a single word or unusual phrase — that jolts and transports the reader from being a casual consumer of literary distractions to suddenly seeing the world anew or from afar. What first appeared slight or mundane is, with a lyrical twist, rendered profound, disorienting, haunting, or even sublime. Moments are extracted from the flow of life and attended to of their own accord, and in a new light. The poet is akin to the fossicking prospector, sifting silt and sand in search of the gold nuggets that lie patiently under our unknowing noses. She is dedicated to uncovering the unseen and unnoticed. She lifts and beats the carpets upon which we tread each day in less than blissful ignorance (for even sneezing is a form of recognition).

While the poet has a reputation for being dreamy and distant, her apparent distraction is in fact a symptom of deeper attention to the pulse of things. She reads between the lines of quotidian life in an attempt to find beauty in humdrum description or exposition. Where no beauty can be found, she takes it upon herself to fabricate some out of nothing. Once upon a time, in the age of Sappho, it is likely that the poet did not need to work so hard to extract such aesthetic pleasures from daily experience, since lyricism had not yet been banished from the lands.[1] (Though it was only

---

1   Sappho's poetry was so powerful that it can still move people today, even when only three or four words have survived the merciless eraser of time. (Though it's also true that such people tend to be pre-primed for such transport through a hyper-sensitivity to poetic flight, to the extent that certain souls go into ecstasy at the furtive offering of a single instance of Sapphic punctuation. What bliss, to be able to swoon at the mere mention of a specific comma or hyphen, covered with the dust and rust of millennia.)

two centuries later that Plato expelled all poets from his ideal republic, since they are apt to distract the good and moral folk with oblique fancies and the seductive "sweet influence" of melody and rhythm.)

If the prose writer provides a substantial meal — the classic meat and two veg of the English Sunday lunch — then the poet offers a subtle, multicourse omakase, each tiny bowl containing a universe of flavors, fragrances, textures, and pungent umami epiphanies. In the age of the professional MFA degree, however, we encounter many prose writers masquerading as poets, attempting to bend a straightforward sentence into something more esoteric simply by impersonating the form of the stanza. Line breaks, however, no matter how strategic, do not create lyricism or poetic effect (though they do require greater attention from the reader, which is a nice trick to oblige them to slow their literary roll).

When all is said and done, the poet continues to say and do things, since she intuitively understands that communication is not really about content — not really about the "what" — but about style and the "how" (what historian Hayden White famously called "the content of the form"). The poet bites her tongue so as not to say the obvious, the banal, the expected, the commonplace (and sometimes she bites so hard she has no choice but to write in blood, or at least to speak with reddened teeth). The poet renders the phatic emphatic by virtue of her musical understanding of human expression.

She holds the shell of life to her ear, and rather than say, "I hear the sound of the ocean," she channels and transcribes the precise whooshing sound of the waves.

The Historian

The historian pays attention to traces, tracks, inscriptions, and transcriptions. She best not be allergic to dust, for she spends many hours in the gloom of cellars, libraries, and storerooms (even as more and more archives "migrate" online, carried on the backs of digital camels — a long caravan forming an orderly exodus along the new Silk Road of the Internet). The historian may be likened to a time-traveling detective, rummaging through manuscripts, logbooks, registries, museums, attics, phone books, and banking records in search of forensic evidence of lives lived, loved, and lost. The historian is preoccupied not only with "what happened" in the past, but with of all those mysterious forces and elements that constitute what we call "the past" in the first place. (After all, much of the past is still very much with us in the present. Just look in your wardrobe for confirmation of this anachronistic fact.)[1] The historian thus pays attention to that mysterious persistence — as much spiritual as material, as much a haunting as an inventory — known as *history*.

For as long as our species has pondered its own origins, history has been a live issue, even as it would take millennia upon millennia to congeal into a discipline and a profession. One might venture that history "proper" began as folktales told around the communal fire, as the next generation were

---

1   Kevin Lynch, *What Time Is This Place?* (Cambridge, MA: MIT Press, 1972).

taught details of great battles and other epic events. These in turn helped illustrate how the ways of the present link back to the destinies and decisions of the before-times. Certainly, the folktale itself would stretch out of shape as it was passed from person to person, and from group to group, succumbing to the "telephone effect" long before the invention of said device. (Indeed, what is history if not an epic game of telephone?) Once the key technology of writing was invented and such stories could be set down in stone, their capacity to morph and evolve surprisingly continued as they shifted from one textual record to the next, trying on different clothing and voices, slipping from place to place and language to language.

For a long time "the great man" model of history held sway, as historians presumed that charisma and genius were the twin engines of human events. For many centuries, chroniclers of times past thus adopted a policy of *cherchez l'homme* on the understanding that epochal changes were always forced or decreed by solitary personalities (even when, as happened with Queen Elizabeth or Joan of Arc, the man turned out to be a woman). But as history accumulated, and historians multiplied, other approaches were explored, and history "itself" – whatever that might actually mean, or include – was more self-consciously processed into a genre, now known as "historiography" (that is, the *writing* of history, as distinct from historical events themselves). Slowly, preservers of the past admitted — to themselves as much as their readers — that the historian was also a storyteller, as in the times before writing. And in order to fit the exigencies of narrative, many a corner had to be smoothed out, or remade altogether, in order to create a coherence that perhaps had no resemblance to the happenings themselves. Suddenly there was a rift between those who loved history for the lessons it imparted to the present ("the moral of the story") and those who loved it simply because it had occurred, for no obvious didactic reason. This in turn meant that the historian was now obliged to pay attention not only to the presumed protagonists of the action, but to the bit players, the second stringers, the understudies, the extras, and even the props. Almost any artifact could become a source, sometimes even in the sense of an informant. And if many still insisted that "history is written by the victors," this was all the more reason to read between the lines in an attempt to excavate the silenced voices of the vanquished.

Today we are all amateur historians in the sense that we create and consult archives (though we may simply call them "keepsakes" or "the bottom kitchen drawer"). From our great-grandparents' love letters, to our children's first finger paintings, to a hidden computer folder called "1980s *Playboy* scans," history persists in many different forms, tones, and colors. Indeed, once you live past a certain age, you are not only a historian by default, in terms of the "oral histories" preserved in your not necessarily reliable memories, but you are also an instance of living history itself. The older you become, the more you drag the baggage of the past with you, to the point that senior citizens become the bent-backed Sherpas of times gone by.

Even young people understand this intuitively, in an age dedicated to a seemingly infinite present, when recent fashions can be dismissed as "so five minutes ago" (itself a phrase from the distant neon past of the early 1990s). Today, "history" is considered to be one giant Tumblr page in which JFK, Genghis Khan, Prohibition, the Crusades, and Cleopatra all rub shoulders on the same flat and irrelevant temporal plane, plundered more for "aesthetic" inspiration than considered in the light of their own contexts, triumphs, and tribulations. Indeed, this postmodern symptom – of feeling trapped in the suffocating amber of an eternal present – has given rise to its own suitably suggestive field of inquiry — "hauntology" (a term that comes to us from Mark Fisher's remix of Jacques Derrida's writings on time and its increasing tendency to fall "out of joint").[2]

As Karl Marx himself noted, "The tradition of all dead generations weighs like a nightmare on the brains of the living."[3] And this weight has multiplied exponentially in an age which now affords us the technical capacity to fix each other's likenesses in haunted liquid crystals called photographs or digital images. New media has created a Cambrian explosion of historical traces — including intimate records of voices, bodies, expressions, gestures, and so on — which leads to a kind of cultural exhaustion.[4] Even as the past grows and grows, it does not create enough mass or momentum to push

---

2   Classic references here are Jacques Derrida, *Specters of Marx* (London: Routledge, 1994); Mark Fisher, *Ghosts of My Life* (Winchester, UK: Zero books, 2014); Walter Benjamin's backward-facing "angel of history," in his "Theses on the Philosophy of History"; and Fredric Jameson's oft-paraphrased observation that, "it is easier to imagine the end of the world than to imagine the end of capitalism." (From his article, "Future City," in *New Left Review*, no.21, May/June, 2003.)

3   Karl Marx, *The Eighteenth Brumaire of Louis Bonaparte* (Chicago: Charles Kerr & Co., 1913). Originally published in 1852.

4   For two especially affecting aesthetic meditations on the hauntology of media, see Bill Morrison's 2002 film *Decasia*, and William Basinski's melancholic album series *The Disintegration Loops*.

us into the future (where "the future" signifies some sense of social or cultural progress).[5]

And yet, tomorrow *does* eventually come, even if it looks depressingly similar to today (which itself looks depressingly similar to 2002, which looked depressingly similar to 1989 and so on). In the aftermath of the crumbling of the Berlin Wall, the Twin Towers, and the American imperial eagle in general — not to mention the rise of the strange new plague that recently ravaged the globe, and the rapid return of the bejeweled Chinese dragon — any claims about "the end of history" seem quaint and naïve.[6] No doubt, what looks like stagnation to the living will look like a dynamic dance toward whatever fate awaits, and which will seem obvious, to the not-yet-born. Climate change, and the existential dangers associated with it, will ensure that the story of humanity continues to change with it, and will no doubt deliver a rather dark message in the process.

The historian is thus another paradoxical figure: trained, like a professional Proustian, to pay attention to the details of lost time for the general edification of future generations, she is a custodian of Time itself. A quiver for Zeno's arrow. And yet, we — as a species — have become increasingly convinced

---

5   No wonder there are currently so many conferences and classes dedicated to becoming "historians of the present."

6   Francis Fukuyama is the name most associated with this now ridiculed idea. I would argue, however, that there is still something compelling and correct in the original diagnosis of this unprecedented age and its inability to even *conceive* of a proper and more just future, let alone to try to design and engineer one. (See also Jean Baudrillard's insistence that we are living, as a society, "after the orgy.")

that we may not have much time left. (And even if we do somehow manage to fabricate a future for ourselves, it is an open question whether we will still have the comprehension skills to read and understand the history books that survive.) Thanks to the "post-typographic" currents and biases of our mediascape, history may once again, as Marshall McLuhan famously argued, become a largely oral affair. This is to say, we may well soon be telling epic stories of our ancestors around the fire — albeit a fire flickering inside an abandoned, rusty oil drum — as we pick the feathered bones of the owl of Minerva from our gray and greasy teeth.

The Judge

The judge pays attention to anything and everything that offers itself up to be judged. He also takes note of all those facts, factors, and details that attempt to flee the harsh light of judgment. He is expected to pay special heed to the evidence, and the protocols for asserting an effective legal argument, and to ignore the cheap suit of the defendant or the nervous facial tic of the prosecutor. He is expected to read between the lines of the case, noticing which statements chime with the evidence and which are deployed in order to distract from the same. He attends to the complex relationship between narrative, logic, memory, conjecture, hearsay, and material traces of the crime. The judge parses all of these elements into a coherent portrait of innocence or culpability (unless the whole thing is derailed by a mistrial; that is, a failure to pay attention to the right procedures).

The judge — as a social, political, historical figure — tends to be a stern middle-aged man, authorized by the power of the state to pass judgment on his fellow men, up to and including the taking of someone's life. As such, the judge's attention is one of the most hallowed, and feared, forms of taking notice. The judge is thus a secular officer of God, doing the kind of work that monotheism was primarily designed to do, but now in a more outsourced, bureaucratic, juridical frame of reference. He is a descendent of St. Peter, only this time in reverse, filling the infernal prisons with the guilty rather than granting paradisiacal access to the innocent. Consequently, a strong whiff of theology clings to the judge's cloak, just as a slight echo of God's thunderous wrath can be heard in the decisive striking of the courtly gavel.

We must also acknowledge, however, that sitting in judgment is not just a formidable vocation, or necessary social function, but also a reflex habit we *all* indulge in, countless times a day. Before we even learn to talk, we learn to make judgments between things we encounter — toys, pets, potential sources of food — perhaps even judging one breast against the other as we suckle at our mother's lactose-rich font. And before we enter young adulthood, we learn to judge each other's bodies, faces, gestures, accents, characters, interests, decisions, and social stations. As we advance through life, we continue to judge each other's taste in clothes, in music, in food, in friends, in "politics," and so on, ad infinitum. Indeed, no instruction is more gleefully ignored than the one that states, "Judge not, lest ye be judged." Rather, we say, "Judge me, sucker, I dare you!… So I can better judge your own poor judgment!" (What is Twitter if not a pretentious piñata of private judgments pretending to pass as a public sphere?) Certainly, we love nothing more than gawping at others from the relative safety of our digital atria, having already lobbed a few rocks in the same direction.[1]

We like to think that our own judgment is the result of rational, objective, hard-won experience and expertise. It would be closer to the truth, however, to say that judgment is almost always a fluctuating jumble of ideology, education,

---

1   As Dolly Parton sings: "If you live in a glass house don't throw stones / Don't shatter my image 'til you look at your own / Look at your reflection in your house of glass / Don't open my closet if your own's full of trash."

cultural baggage, neurological wiring, the last thing you read on the Internet, weather, optics, presumption, blood sugar levels, pheromones, personal taste (or, more often, *dis*taste[2]), and an almost infinite list of contextual cues, both ambient and overdetermined. As Jane Austen understood so well, most judgment is in fact a form of prejudice (which itself is a form of pride).

Not all judgments need be judgmental, however. They can also involve more neutral decisions concerning balance, timing, force, direction, and other factors spanning the measurable to the ineffable. (As the old joke notes, Italian women know precisely how much seasoning or herbs to put in a dish because the ghosts of their maternal ancestors whisper to them from the other side: "*Basta così* — that's enough.") We make such instinctual judgments all the time, from when to "pop the question" to when we should pop a pimple. This is to say, every decision — of which we make tens of thousands in a day — involves some form of judgment. Most of these, however, are semi-conscious at best. The type that concerns us here, however, involves the full scope of our attentional capacities, and can further be broadly divided into two subtypes: the aesthetic (concerning the realm of art) and the ethical (concerning the realm of proper behavior).

If we consider the artist — creating her work, in her chosen medium — the judge is already present in her process, choosing between options and narrowing down the shapeless and unwieldy muse of possibility into the defiant totem of actual, polished expression. If we then consider the art lover, experiencing the same creative work with open-mindedness,

---

2   "There is an erotics of dislike" — John Lanchester, *The Debt to Pleasure* (London: Picador, 1996), p. 12.

the judge is even more conspicuous in the foreground, weighing the evidence for its beauty, provocation, or relevance, and pronouncing a verdict — either in print or simply to oneself — about the work's artistic merit (usually measured by the degree to which we feel the work rewards the gift of our own attention). When it comes to ethics, the judge is similarly poised to deliver a verdict, only in this case it refers to the behavior of a person, character, or even country. Rather than assessing the enigmatic quality of a non-utilitarian object, the judge is here concerned with a kind of moral calculus.

Strangely, we have reached a cultural moment when much of our aesthetic output is judged primarily, if not exclusively, on the extent to which it explicitly signals a statement on ethics. The two independent registers have merged. For most of human history, art has been produced in order to either *reflect* the world or to create a parallel space in which to explore the complexity and ambiguity of human deeds and motives. Today, however, we find ourselves in an unprecedented time (foreshadowed by the sentimental, hypocritical Victorians, to be sure) when art is obliged to answer a swift cross-examination in the dock before being deemed worthy and forthright enough to be released into public life (and even then, the jury of public opinion reserves the right to a new appeal at any moment, with the result that the work of art is forever on parole).

Such an intimate dynamic between art and ethics reinforces the structural power of the judge, who enjoys an exceptional position and numinous sphere of influence that does not, for all that, correspond to any specific stamp of his person or any particular corner of the content of his character. In other words, no matter how dull — or even how contemptible — the judge happens to be as an individual, as soon as he puts on the official robes of his office, he also drapes himself in the infallible authority of God's representative on earth (as evidenced in the confirmation process of almost every supreme court judge in modern history). Beyond this question of social hierarchy, however, there is a *metaphysical asymmetry* between the judge and the one being judged that we should take into account, a disproportion that is invisibly embodied in the figure of the so-called Big Other.

Who exactly is the Big Other? He is the phantasmatic amalgam of everyone you fear pronouncing judgment upon you. He is an impossible, nightmarish composite of father, priest, boss, teacher, cop, and every other despot you are likely to meet — as capable of affording you the relief of social approval as he is likely to capriciously reject you for some undefined crime (such as simply existing without a permit). No single individual can map one-to-one onto the shadowy figure of the Big Other. Specific people encountered in one's life, however, can lend some disturbing details to the portraits of this looming alterity that your own psyche loves to draw in the dark corners of your mind (like a disturbed child locked in the attic for an endless rainy afternoon). Over the span of our lives, we audition dozens of people to be our own personal Big Other — a crush, a therapist, a coach, a director, a critic, and so on. But none can fully measure up to the abstract fear that the Big Other–shaped hole in our psyche creates. (If our demanding professor suddenly dies, for instance, there is another judgmental understudy to take his place.)

This is the terrifying lesson of Kafka's bleak novel *The Trial*, in which K. is held forever in the suspended judgment of a verdict which never comes. The Big Other stays, appropriately, out of the picture, since his power is that of the "structuring absence": the withering, devastating judgment asymptotically delivered by someone with no face, and thus with no legible place where one can negotiate an appeal or plea for mercy. The Big Other is the only one whose judgment we are truly afraid of, and thus the one who influences our own judgment most profoundly (since we have internalized them in an act of anticipation that also works as an act of inoculation). We judge the world from the perspective of the one we think will judge us the most harshly, and thus whose judgment we value most highly.

Hence the enduring popularity of reality TV. The genius of this toxic, addictive genre resides in the perverse power of "the judges" — Paul Hollywood, Nigel Lythgoe, Heidi Klum, Simon Cowell... the list is endless. And no matter how frivolous or fallible the celebrity sitting in judgment, the structure of the competition allows such profane figures to occupy the untouchable position of the Big Other (at least for the duration of the show). The judge is not simply a critic, or an anointed expert, but again, a kind of demi-god (as is made most explicit in the fleeting cooking competition *Crazy Delicious*, in which the judges are dressed in white and inhabit the cloudlike heavens).

Perhaps it's unfair to emphasize the *structure* of televisual judgment at the expense of the genuine expertise and training that these judges bring with them on set, and the kind of focused, pedagogic attention that some of them, at least, bring to bear on whatever object they are being paid to assess. Gastronomic judges, for instance, are certainly paying attention to everything set on the table before them, from presentation, to texture, to fragrance, to flavor, to the holistic concept that binds all the ingredients together. They are enlisting all their senses and more in their placement of the meal on the spectrum from inedible to transcendent. Which is all to say that the judge is another ambivalent figure — part mentor, part bully — who can at one moment inspire us to do our very best, and in the next moment discourage us from even trying ever again. (And here we should also note those strange pseudo-sports — like ice-skating, gymnastics, high diving, and so on — that depend on the subjective and selective attention of a panel of judges to simulate objective measures of excellence.)

Ultimately, no matter how fearsome the one assessing our actions, we suspect that we judge ourselves more harshly than others will. Indeed, many of us tend to be our own worst critics (or, at least, we like to *think* we are, whereas in practice, our self-sentencing is often simply suspended, pending further evidence, or passed with breathtaking leniency). Meanwhile, the judge continues to inhabit the upholstered chambers of our own minds, consulting his leatherbound books on etiquette, ethics, and other Byzantine nuances of interpersonal jurisprudence. As a result, our inner monologue all too often devolves into the cynical rhetoric of the lawyer, pandering to the ladies and gentleman of the jury. ("Your honor," we cry, citing all sorts of mitigating circumstances. "The ice-cream container was already open!") We judge ourselves so that others may, hopefully, contradict our own findings and negotiate a plea bargain, if not a reprieve.

The attention of the judge thus saturates every stratum and aspect of society, creating an entire population of second-guessers, a whole species of legal secretaries. What might happen, however, if we learned to not only suspend, but *reject* our compromised, less than generous judgments? What might replace the shrewd cocking of the head, the stroking of the chin, and the sadistic jouissance of the verdict? Could we pay more attention to the aesthetic process, rather than to its reified, rather lonely end product and the humble lessons and collaborations it allows? Might we deftly sidestep the rehearsed, lead-footed moral choreography of capital-E Ethics in order to improvise a more soft-shoe shuffle of mischievous mutual recognition?

In other words, explicitly describing the over-coded attention economy of the judge — the practiced decision trees of condemnation or clemency — is perhaps the first step toward deposing the tyranny of the Big Other, along with the ambitious entourage of medium-sized alter egos that cluster around him (compare *Mean Girls*). Such impractical fantasies of a life without judgment are, of course, naïve at best. Though perhaps there are worse fates than to be accused of indulging in daydreams in which people thrive in a world where they are, even to themselves, innocent before proven guilty.

The Curator

The curator pays attention to tiny, orphaned signals swirling like dust particles within the churning clamor of the world. She sorts wheat from chaff, sheep from goats, and men from boys (in a context where the latter term outnumbers the former by many orders of magnitude, according to the traditional hay/needle ratio). The quintessential curator works for a museum or gallery, selecting the elements that will make the best impression on visitors, either in terms of aesthetics or edification, ideally both. Sometimes the curator is like a dowser trying to detect a rumored subterranean stream beneath the limestone. At other times, she is like a bowerbird, selecting shiny and attractive items previously scattered to the four winds. At other times still, she is like Maxwell's famous demon straining to catch and separate slow-moving molecules from fast in a bid to outsmart the zealous natural forces of decay (and in truth, her task has a similar aim, attempting to transcend the ennui of entropy via the psycho-spiritual torque of selective enthusiasm). The curator is a conductor of affinities, both overt and secret. She isolates flows among the mass — or masses among the flow — depending on the objects being sought and the rationale for placing them together under the same rubric.

Once upon a time, the curator was guardian of a small world, shepherding disparate elements into a cabinet of curiosities. This latter was composed of miscellaneous items connected by no theme or logic beyond the operative curiosity itself. A special pleasure was gleaned in curating such exhibits for the delight and caprice of all those who attended to them, since they bestowed a certain value on each singular object by virtue of the resonance created between them (a resonance often created by nothing other than proximity within a single collection or space). The curator of centuries past was preoccupied with assembling a set of elements that could whisper to each other long after the visitors had left and the candles had been snuffed out. What stories they told no doubt detailed not only their origins, but the crooked journey and adventures they had endured since. Before the Industrial Revolution, when most things were made by hand or with rudimentary tools, objects had more "personality," charm, presence, and even aura. They forged a kind of intimacy, partly because the world had not yet filled every niche and crevice with aggressively generic and materialized *stuff*.

Today, however, the curator faces a different challenge (or the same challenge, but at a much different scale, which in turn changes the nature of the game). In an age addicted to disposability and planned obsolescence, the task becomes less to find singular objects to heed and listen to than to make most of the crap *go away*.[1] Where once upon a time the curator was required to make a judgment between the quality of two signals, the problem today is to somehow briefly bracket off the noise of late industrial capitalism and the overdeveloped economy. Indeed, some people make good money as consultants distilling a million viable options down to a short list of two or three. Never mind the pseudo-science or new age voodoo required to perform such a task; the clients are happy to pay for the now clear pathway

---

1   I owe this point to McKenzie Wark, in conversation.

through the mountains of *merde*. Nevertheless, the same skill set applies today as it did from the earliest of times, when the Egyptian pharaohs hired consultants to decide which artifacts and relics would best represent their sacred status to the gods beyond the sun.

The curator, in essence, is an active instance of the connoisseur, using her discerning eye and practiced judgment to definitively gather elements together, rather than simply appreciating — or rejecting — things as they come. The curator thus lives or dies on the reputation of her taste, opinion, and expertise. As any nineteenth-century Parisian socialite worth her salt knew, deep in her calcium-rich bones, the most important thing one can curate is *people*. We usually curate our social circles, our useful acquaintances — and indeed our frenemies — with a more studied eye than our intimate friends; though some even hold unspoken auditions and annual performance reviews for the latter. Wardrobes, bookshelves, record collections, fruit bowls, refrigerators, vacations, and vaccinations... anything and everything can be curated. (As one startup CEO says to another in the satirical TV show *Silicon Valley*: "The first thing you gotta do? Get a good fruit guy.") Indeed, we are constantly sold the message that we should be actively *curating* our lives rather than merely, passively, leading them. Today, even something as intangible as an experience is best approached via the curation process (God forbid a modern person be exposed to an *uncurated* one).

The term "curate" comes from the Latin word for "care," suggesting a strong therapeutic legacy. The curator indeed pays attention to things worthy of care, just as she cares for the things she pays attention to. Such care can turn into an unhealthy obsession, however, if she tries to curate every aspect of her life and leave nothing to chance, serendipity, or even the often wise forces of chaos. The curator, in fact, abhors chaos, just as nature abhors a vacuum, and her entire raison d'être is assembled around the need to find, create, and maintain order in a universe that seems to enjoy pranking the very idea of such. In contrast to the absurd anti-laws of quantum physics and the random spectacle of human affairs, the curator is almost a religious figure (and recall here the historical role of the curate). As a consequence, she follows humbly in the footsteps of Our Lord, who curated the world into existence. (Not a bad trick — curating something out of literally nothing!)

In the digital age, anyone with a YouTube channel or Pinterest board is, practically by default, a curator. Strangely, perhaps even ironically, there seems to be an arms race between human curators and cybernetic ones. We now trust the algorithm to recommend things and thus spare us the trouble of sorting through the chaos almost as much as we trust a friend or expert. A successful curator has a sixth sense for not only *what* they curate, but *who* they are curating for (even if it's just for themselves). In this regard, the algorithm has an advantage since it can watch us — and listen to us (and analyze us) — 24/7. Uncannily, the recommendation engines often seem to understand us better than we understand ourselves, suggesting things that we didn't realize we wanted or needed. (Of course, this is a neat capitalist trick, using "nudges" to train us into *thinking* we wanted a pressure cooker or a Peloton all along — when we could well have done without it.)[2] The personal curator is thus a potential hero-rebel figure,

---

2   See the brilliant blog posts written by Rob Horning at https://thenewinquiry.com/blogs/marginal-utility/

utilizing organic, authentic, human faculties and skills in the service of a better or more interesting life, and against the cold, compromised computations of machine learning. But sadly, the curator too often hobbles behind Amazon or Netflix in assembling listicles that will have an influence on the attention economy writ large.

But what did we expect in an age when things have evolved into commodities and — as Marx foretold — any given table may start standing on its head and "dancing of its own free will"? It becomes more difficult to curate a cabinet of curiosities when the curiosities themselves go rogue and start smashing the glass doors to find their own freedom. The curator is now obliged to treat her own life as a commodity, or at least as a brand. She curates social media feeds in a way that excludes anything potentially controversial, undesirable, or boring (or too revealing of her actual existence). As such, like the influencer, the curator pays extra attention to the vicissitudes and whimsy of the algorithm. She tries to anticipate its moods and modulations in order to maximize her chances of being blessed by maximum exposure and given a prime position in the infinite scroll. And in this sense, she is working to please the Big Other of social media itself: a monstrous chimera stitching together the algorithmic sorting engine and the gestalt potential of global eyeballs. In the days before the Internet, the curator had to anticipate the blessing of the art world or its equivalent. Her Big Other was the press and the various reviews and receptions of her collecting capacities. But this has reached exponential proportions as she second-guesses attempts to please the people and the bots at one and the same time.

Indeed, the curator is conflicted about her own instincts to collect, arrange, and order. She wonders if it's really worth telling a story through the juxtaposition of objects or images. She still gets some kind of thrill from being the organizing principle behind a set of elements presented to the world within a certain frame or on a specific platform. But secretly, in her heart of hearts, she wants to free the objects and let them jumble themselves up — to run riot. She dreams of chaff-infused wheat, sheepish goats, and a necklace of hay threaded through a stack of needles. For, just as the surrealist writer Comte de Lautréamont experienced a delicious shiver when he came upon a sewing machine placed randomly next to an umbrella, the curator's soul is freed by the haphazard, the erratic, and the arbitrary. She understands that life itself is the ultimate curator, and no considered plan or narrative frame can rival the sheer prodigious force of the contingency of Being.

And so, after the exhibit has closed for the night, the curator goes home, and at least in her dreams, she surrenders to unexpected, unruly — even *undeserved* — conjunctions.

The Architect

The architect pays attention to the ways in which space can be converted into place. When planning a new building, he considers not only the physical topography of the land, but the aspect, setting, charge, and sociocultural context. In this sense, he must balance the needs of everything from the soil, to the client, to the seasonal trajectory of the sun, to the political Zeitgeist, to the often diva-like requirements of the materials used. We tend to think of architects as fundamentally *creative* creatures, making something out of nothing so that we may live, sleep, and work more comfortably. But we may also think of them as strategically destructive, or at least disassembling. The architect parcels the open air into units, and in doing so creates an enclosed potential plenum out of a presumed vacuum. (Humans are not good at acknowledging the presence or integrity of something they cannot see, as is the case with the air, or whatever one might call "the space between things.")[1]

Indeed, from an unexpected perspective, the architect resembles the butcher, carving up the invisible carcass of virtual space into recognizable "cuts" of inhabitable sections. (As historian Carla Nappi notes, "How something comes

---

1   Joe Milutis, *Ether: The Nothing That Connects Everything* (Minneapolis: University of Minnesota Press, 2005).

apart is what makes it what it is.")[2] Just as a pig miraculously becomes pork once it has been killed, cleaned, and cleaved, a previously undesignated area becomes a bedroom, or a kitchen, or a bathroom once it has been captured, enclosed, englobed, and domesticated. Given that much of the world has now already been occupied and reterraformed, in some sense, the architect is no longer so concerned with pulling three-dimensional structures up out of a tabula rasa like a sophisticated pop-up book. Instead, he is usually asked to renovate and rejuvenate an abode that has started to show its age one way or another, either through modest wear and tear or through sheer neglect and full-scale abandonment.

At the origins of humanity, we find traces of humble dwellings improvised out of the soil, clay, sand, or snow; structures inherited like recipes, and as organic as a tree. As civilizations developed — Chinese, Egyptian, Aztec — civic or sacred structures became more elaborate and called for special technologies and proficiencies. Enter the expertise of the architect and his intimate understanding of the relationship between the rather random location of the self and the fixed and fateful workings of the cosmos, a relationship that can be mapped and measured, and then literally set in stone. The architect can be forgiven, then, for a certain amount of hubris. After all, his calling is not too remote from the divine accomplishment of God, who made the world in six days. Deliberately and meticulously creating something from nothing is a consecrated mandate, especially when it is the type of *something* which transcends a mere object and becomes an

---

2   Carla Nappi, *Translating Modern China: Illegible Cities* (Cambridge, UK: Cambridge University Press, 2021), p. 220.

environment: a place which we inhabit and entrust with our most intimate experiences.

Even at the prosaic level of everyday experience, the architect makes decisions that impact every aspect of our lives, since he decides who sleeps where and next to whom. He thus renders power dynamics into physical structures (even more visibly when it comes to public buildings like schools, clinics, and prisons, as Foucault well understood). The architect ostensibly adapts apertures and angles to the needs of people, but in practice it is more often the other way around. He is tempted to put the needs of the building first as he channels stone, wood, and steel into configurations that please him and his creation, while the inhabitants must adjust to sharp corners, cold corridors, or mystifying, Escheresque staircases. The architect has the power to make demi-gods of his clients through panoramic windows or towering aspects. Conversely, he has the ability to humble us, depending on the proximity we are obliged to maintain to the various odors and noises of human ablutions.

Once again, the architect is a kind of quasi-shamanic figure, in tune with cosmic ligaments and universal ley lines. (One need only look at the iconography and literature of the Freemasons to understand the esoteric lineage linking the pyramids of ancient Egypt with the McMansions of Central New Jersey.) Even if staunchly secular and scientific, the architect applies his own sense of what the Chinese call feng shui, welcoming — through the gravity-defying techniques of his craft — the spirits of fresh air, or banishing the demons of poor insulation. He is a diplomat, shuttling between the needs and eccentricities of his materials and the invisible infrastructure of the universe. The architect thus attempts to forge metaphysics into physics.

Indeed, it is tempting to think of the architect less as a prime mover, reshaping the world according to personal will, than as a channeler of cosmic forces, shepherding yet-unrealized patterns and forms — waiting patiently in the wings of the world, as it were — into actuality. He is the medium for material manifestation, as new structures assemble themselves, through his mind and blueprints, into existence (just as, from this Deleuzian perspective, planes are the crystallization of the virtual line linking London and New York across the Atlantic, or Frenchmen are merely the belated invention of primal shrugs, which needed a conducive medium through which to become real and palpable). As such, the architect pays attention to the grain of any given place or structure, from the tiniest block of wood to the largest ornamental flourish. And he does so in order to create something either in harmony with its surroundings and its inhabitants, or something in deliberate defiance of its local context — the territorial terror of its *terroir*.

In his epic three-volume history of human ontology *qua* topology, *Spheres*, German philosopher Peter Sloterdijk notes that humans are a species that requires post-utero cocoons in order to orient and conduct their lives. "Shelter" has always been instinctively understood as the primary prerequisite and premise for any subsequent kind of striving, pleasure, or endeavor. One must be safely housed before all else. (Hence the primal fear, loathing, and pity we have when encountering "the homeless," since they represent the existential void that awaits all of us, when carpets or polished floorboards are suddenly pulled out from under our feet.) For Sloterdijk, however, the sphere is *the* archetypal structure — at once organic and cultural, material and symbolic — englobing the human in psychosocial comfort and protection on the one hand, but also creating the criteria and mechanism of exclusion on the other. "If one had to pinpoint the dominant motif in the metaphysical era of European thought in a single word," Sloterdijk writes, "it could only be 'globalization.'" Why? Because we humans are essentially "orb-creating and orb-inhabiting animals."[3]

The contemporary architect upholds this ancient, Eurocentric legacy of highly measured self-englobing, but does so with a supplemental modern, even cubist, sensibility. What began as smooth and uniform as an egg now sprouts violent angles and disorienting canopies, as if something rather monstrous is finally hatching. He enjoys deconstructing things even more than constructing them. (Or rather, he enjoys tracing the ambivalent dance between deconstruction and reconstruction and then freezing such processes in time as inhabitable structures.) Think of Sydney's famous opera house, for example, which is said to have been inspired by the perfect sphere of an orange, but only after it had been fanned out into segments.

In *The Poetics of Space*, a lyrical meditation on the primal power of *home*, Gaston Bachelard asks, "Of all the houses in which we have found shelter, above and beyond all the houses we have dreamed we live in, can we isolate an intimate, concrete essence that would be a justification of the uncommon value of all our images of protected intimacy?"[4] The romantic Frenchman does not take long in isolating this essence, which he believes to be the "chief benefit of the house," namely that which allows its inhabitant "to dream in peace." For Bachelard,

---

3   Peter Sloterdijk, *Globes: Spheres II* (Los Angeles: Semiotext(e), 2014), p. 45.

4   Gaston Bachelard, *The Poetics of Space* (Boston: Beacon, 1969), p. 3.

then, the dream house is designed explicitly for dreaming. It is a structure that strives upward, in sheer verticality, toward the heavens in order to inspire "the anthropo-cosmic tissue of a human life." Alas, the modern architect has misunderstood his sacred task, and now perpetuates the banal profanity of "mere horizontality." "In Paris there are no houses," Bachelard writes. Instead, "the inhabitants of the big city live in superimposed boxes." He laments the lost wisdom that "the house is a world in itself," and goes on to argue that we must rediscover, and redouble, a conscious effort to honor those "centers of condensation of intimacy" which nurture our bodies, minds, and souls.[5]

Such poetics, however, were waved away impatiently by the next generation — and indeed by Le Corbusier, in his own time — who (with some justification, it must be said) believed them to reek of bourgeois privilege. Instead, the modern architect thinks of the house as "a machine for living in," and of the city itself as a neoclassical ordering of rational lines, much too radiant to suffer the soft lamp glow of shadowy secrets and musty intimacies. The architect can thus scale his powers up, from a single building to an all-encompassing vision. Under the seemingly innocent guise of "landscape architect," "developer," or "city planner," he can fragment, isolate, or abolish entire communities with the stroke of a pen (just as Robert Moses perversely reincarnated his namesake when parting the Manhattan shoreline, separating the city from the Hudson River so that his descendants may flee to Long Island or New Jersey come the end of the workday).

The architect, it must be said, is notorious for dreaming up designs that put enormous pressures on everyone involved in

---

5   Ibid., pp. 26–29.

the construction process, from the structural engineer, who is responsible for ensuring that the building will stay up in most conditions, to the laborer, who must ensure that each idiosyncratic detail, folly, curve, and joinery are adhered to. He is thus often depicted as a tyrant. In Ayn Rand's fascistic romance *The Fountainhead*, architect Howard Roark is portrayed as a heroic figure, "the ideal man," standing up against petty meddling for the sake of his individual vision. Roark even goes so far as to dynamite his project rather than let it take shape in a compromised form. And the novel ends atop his next commission: the aspirational phallic thrust of a skyscraper. As Roark insists:

> Man cannot survive except through his mind. He comes on earth unarmed. His brain is his only weapon. Animals obtain food by force. Man had no claws, no fangs, no horns, no great strength of muscle. He must plant his food or hunt it. To plant, he needs a process of thought. To hunt, he needs weapons, and to make weapons — a process of thought. From this simplest necessity to the highest religious abstraction, from the wheel to the skyscraper, everything we are and we have comes from a single attribute of man — the function of his reasoning mind.[6]

The architect need not, however, remain the avatar of a sovereign, all-too-human world-making will. After all, beavers manage to build elaborate structures, and even "terraform" entire valleys, without, presumably, giving a single individual

---

6   Ayn Rand, *The Fountainhead* (Indianapolis: The Bobbs-Merrill Company, 1943).

all the credit. Ants build elaborate city structures with stratified neighborhoods and sophisticated air-conditioning systems. Bees create geometric structures for their complex toils. And bowerbirds obsess about the aesthetic impact of their constructions, which can be several stories high and surrounded by ornamental gardens.

In short, the architect pays particular attention to our own specific triangulation of building, dwelling, and thinking.[7] A good one takes special note of the needs of his clients, as well as those of the structure itself, the terrain on which it is built, the sociopolitical context in which it was commissioned, and the cosmic trajectories which it extends and crystallizes. A bad one, by contrast, imposes his own will, or the will of his bosses, and thus obliges his inhabitants to adapt to hostile spaces and constricting places like rats inside a Skinner box. Perhaps one need not be as nostalgic as Bachelard to prioritize the importance not only of physical shelter from the elements, but of the creation of spaces which both allow and encourage daydreaming. This in turn yields the immeasurable benefit of nourishing a mind that feels both "at home" *and* in the midst of intergalactic adventures, at one and the same time.

---

7 Martin Heidegger, "Building, Dwelling, Thinking," in *Poetry, Language, Thought* (New York: Harper Colophon Books, 1971).

The Influencer

The influencer pays attention to emerging trends in whatever niche, subculture, milieu, or microsphere she holds sway. This is a tricky balancing act, not least because she needs to promote novelties that have not yet become rote or mundane while at the same time avoiding straying too far from the familiar (lest her followers no longer find such content reassuringly "relatable"). Additionally, the influencer must operate in a dizzying contemporary mediascape, one that has become practically detached from any kind of intelligible, linear narrative about cultural progress. Out of the flotsam and jetsam of life, swirling in the Great Global Garbage Patch of postmodern confusion, she must therefore create her own "story" — one of the most overused words of our time. She must do this, moreover, in order to forge some kind of brand-worthy coherence among all the different styles, signs, attitudes, and "aesthetics" that tumble frantically around us. The influencer herself is thus a conscientious, albeit distracted, *shepherd of attention*, a Little Bo-Peep charged with holding the gaze and interest of her fluctuating flock of fickle sheep. And how does she do this? By turning to other influencers in turn, those working further up the fields or higher up the chain. (The New Age mystics are wrong, in other words, for it's not "turtles all the way down," but influencers.) The influencer is thus responsible for rapid inflation within the attention economy, as more and more people attempt to assert influence over each other, through wildly proliferating platforms.

This new cultural heroine — an evolution of the sexy, smart, urban magazine columnist — is an accomplished *bricoleuse*, turning the world into a giant mood board. She decants dubious wine into new, artisanal bottles. Indeed, the influencer is finely attuned to the ways in which neglected historical leftovers, jammed toward the back of the pop cultural refrigerator, can be efficiently microwaved back into a kind of fleeting, lukewarm relevance (whereby every haircut, hemline, and pop hit must be resuscitated yet again, for the *nth* time, like a bad high-school-musical version of Nietzsche's eternal return). The influencer soon learns, however, that the sheer scale and momentum of real-time feedback from followers is addictive and dangerous. It threatens to turn her inside out, as it were, from a centripetal being — in whom the world flows inward, reinforcing the whorls and architecture of the self — to a centrifugal creature, from whom all the contents of her identity are suddenly flung outward. The influencer thus spins like a top, and requires the same kind of vertiginous physics in order to retain her balance.

The influencer is obsessed with popularity, metrics, and the cruel and capricious decisions of the algorithm. In this sense, she pays attention to her own brand or reputation in the same way a Wall Street trader pays attention to his favorite stocks, experiencing the same butterflies when the numbers dip or waver. Like all narcissists, she is a paradoxical figure, stuck between her own vanity and self-regard, on one side, and the infinite need for validation by others, on the other. Where the poet is a creative witness to the world, the influencer is a slave to the deep human need to be validated or "seen." The influencer fears she may simply disappear — wink into non-existence — if she does not receive the requisite amount of likes or comments. ("Pics or it didn't happen.") She thus instinctively understands the gathering power of the uncanny, anonymous, distributed *witnessing* that the Internet allows. She feels, on a constant and visceral level, the imperative of self-exposure that social media in particular demands, along with the damage it has wrought on our collective sense of place, or placelessness, within it (since we have all but lost the art of being simply in "the here and now," now that every experience must be preempted, preapproved, re-performed, restaged, and reframed for what used to be called "a Kodak moment").[1] The upshot? The influencer is a personification of "The Most Photographed Barn in America" from Don DeLillo's classic novel *White Noise*: a mostly empty thing, whose popularity is purely tautological and self-fulfilling.

One keen irony: the more the influencer craves to be liked and acknowledged, the more she adds to the ubiquitous clamor of networked attempts to attract and secure attention. By participating in this vicious cycle, she becomes just another solitary penny in the vast sorting machine of surveillance capitalism. The more she wants to be recognized as an individual, the more she helps create the conditions for

---

1 Eda Yu: "The inextricable flow of digital technology in our lives has rendered it more difficult than ever to be emotionally connected to our experiences." Moreover, the "cognitive offloading" that occurs when we're more preoccupied with "capturing" the moment, than simply enjoying it often leads to what neuroscientists call the "photo-taking-impairment effect." As the name suggests, the more you ask your camera to remember a moment for you, the less your brain's mnemonic cells feel obliged to actually commit it to memory. Eda Yu, "Instagram and Snapchat Are Ruining Our Memories," Vice, 1 April 2019: https://www.vice.com/en/article/social-media-is-ruining-our-memories-v26n1/

global anonymity, human homogeneity, and the sheer generic "dividualism" of the overdeveloped media age.

But who influences the influencer? Paradoxically, perhaps, the people being influenced by her in the first place, since she lives in fear of displeasing her followers and thus losing her influence. Similar in form to the classic Hegelian master-slave dialectic, the influencer needs the influenced more than the other way around, even if the perceived asymmetry suggests otherwise. Today, the influencer is a living contradiction, paying excessive attention to herself and her own life, but only as a kind of potlatch of her own identity. She breaks herself into a million digital pieces in order to share herself, as a kind of pagan sacrifice, to her followers. And by the same token, the influenc*ed* absorb their digital guides, gurus, and mentors, in a kind of voracious, ambivalent cannibalism.[2]

The influencer tells us, but not in so many words, that we no longer trust ourselves to be the witnesses to the world and our own lives. We need others to affirm we exist, like so many insecure trees toppling in a forsaken forest. What's more, we feel we need to *be* the Event. We need to bask in the aura of That-Which-Others-Fear-They-Are-Missing-Out-On.   We need an army of faceless witnesses in order to feel a sense of our own ontological ballast. ("I post therefore I am.") Social media takes our striving sympathy toward what Heidegger called *Dasein* (truly "being-here"), as well as our profound and innate sense of *Mitsein* (truly "being together"), and turns these into an isolating, bingeable, transactional spectacle: high-calorie, low-nutrient eye candy. Instagram (which would be the perfect name for a cocaine delivery service, by the way) creates a claustrophobic sense of an eternal present —

---

2   Sigmund Freud, *Totem and Taboo* (Boston: Beacon Press, 1913).

an ongoing instantaneity — without stakes, pleasures, or any possibility of progress. It is important to resist this infectious stagnation, however, and push back against what Mark Fisher called "the slow cancellation of the future." Moreover, it is important to pay attention to things beyond what the algorithm wants us to notice (otherwise we aren't really paying attention, but merely being led by the nose).

It is no coincidence that the influencer has become such a central cultural figure at the same moment that stable, salaried jobs — especially for younger people — have essentially evaporated altogether. The new generation can no longer count on traditional trades, apprenticeships, or vocations, so they must instead attempt to make a monetizable impression on the world through their own resources. For conventionally attractive young women especially, this means aspiring to become a one-person fashion brand: acting as model, make-up artist, stylist, PA, photographer, and publicist all at once. In the ever-scrolling, aspirational worlds opened up by Instagram and TikTok, the attention economy is intimately entwined with the political one, both increasingly invested in channeling vast amounts of wealth up toward those who already have more capital than most countries. (Because the mega-wealthy apparently don't have enough space yachts yet.) Indeed, we might note in passing that today's unprecedented wealth-hoarding — usually described in the press under the more anodyne name of "disparity" — is a key consequence of a reckless and inhumane experiment to find out *just how far* any kind of social safety net, or civic-minded structure whatever, can be removed, Jenga-style, before the whole thing collapses into a miserable heap. And if we take this wider context into account, the polished and pixel-plumped smile of the Instagram influencer starts to look less like a cute solicitation, and more like the desperate death mask of our gangrenous necrocracy.

The influencer has the potential, at least, to lead us — Moses style — out of the shimmering mirages of the desert of the hyperreal. After all, in hindsight, some of the most important activists and radical thinkers throughout history were "influencers," in an expanded, non-branded sense. Not long ago, it wouldn't have been a stretch to call Bernie Sanders one, as measured in memes alone. The same goes for Greta Thunberg in terms of "impact." Thousands of today's political organizers and intellectual dissidents are poaching the tricks and techniques of fashionistas and wellness gurus in an effort to drag collective attention toward the real issues that matter: the climate emergency, the labor crisis, structural prejudice, and so on. In our highly mediated attention ecology, the "anxiety of influencers" can be transformed, leading us to finally face up to the influence of shared, legitimate anxieties.

The Factory Worker

The factory worker pays attention to the needs and caprices of the factory itself. She must therefore adapt strictly to those objects, rules, and rituals that the production process deems most important, especially the machines used in the manufacturing process. As Charlie Chaplin illustrated so vividly in his classic film *Modern Times*, the factory worker is obliged to hang up the extraneous aspects of her humanity along with her coat and insert herself into the gears and levers of the assembly line. She becomes either an integral part of the machine's machinations, or simply a watcher of the machine, intervening when something goes awry. The attention of the factory worker is usually specific and relentless: the turning of a single bolt, over and over again; the stitching of a single hem; the sealing of a single cap. Twentieth-century techniques — now called Fordist, in honor of Henry Ford's early automobile factories — pioneered the assembly line model, in which an army of hyper-focused workers are each responsible for a particular, isolated element of the final product.[1] This often meant that workers were both highly specialized and low-skilled. Any able-bodied person, no matter how slow out of

---

1   It is often noted that Henry Ford lifted this idea from the vast Chicago slaughterhouses, which allocated different men to carve up different parts of the cows, pigs, and chickens. This is to say, Ford's famous assembly line was inspired by the Midwestern *dis*-assembly line.

the gate, could be trained to do a specific manual movement, over and over again, like an especially resigned monkey.[2]

This scenario plays havoc with the attention span and the attention economy, since the factory worker is obliged to become a warm-blooded robot, watching the conveyer belt with a concentrated efficiency and a crisp lack of superfluous gestures. Of course, things can vary wildly from factory to factory. Cuban cigar factories, for instance, may *possibly* have been as lively and convivial as some sweaty portraits in highly exoticized 1950s Hollywood movies, though I would not want to press the point (especially to someone who actually worked in one). But overall, and very much increasingly so, the factory worker is obliged to keep their head down, their eyes focused, their mouths shut, their hands at the ready, and their minds on the mind-numbing job. Ironically, perhaps — or at least as a consequence — this industrialized monotony, clattering behind the scenes of our economy, creates the ideal conditions for distraction and daydreaming. An endless carousel of candy, corduroy, cans, or computer chips only serves to blur the thinking process. So while the hands may remain nimble, the mind can wander, replaying last night's movie, argument, or romantic encounter. Here lies, however, the source of so many industrial accidents, in which a factory worker may lose anything from her poise, to her nail, to her finger, to her life, to her will to live. (We are now familiar with

2   My father claims that his first job was supervising a conveyer belt of passing pies before the pastry lids were secured on top. The pies passed beneath an industrial fan that would frequently suck in passing birds, and his job was to remove any conspicuous bones and feathers before the upper crust was applied. I should add, however, that my father is prone to fanciful exaggerations.

the horror stories emerging from the Foxconn factories in China, in which many of our electronic devices are produced and assembled, and where strategically placed nets have been installed to discourage workers' suicide attempts.)

These days, factory work is being increasingly outsourced to robots. Indeed, we see more and more factories creating machines that then promptly go to work creating more machines *ad infinitum*. Except for the occasional lonely overseer or night watchman, the factory is self-assembling. Indeed, the idea of a human employee in a processing plant is quite quaint. Instead, our species is now required to do the labor in the warehouses and distribution plants.[3] Robots have yet to master the improvised dexterity of the primate's opposable thumb, so — for the moment at least — human factory workers are required in the vast and multitudinous clearinghouses of Amazon and Alibaba. In contrast to the specific vigil they were obliged to endure a generation or two before, today's factory workers do not even enjoy this soporific, soul-destroying luxury. Instead they are fitted out with apps, tracking mechanisms, and augmented technics, all of which combine to render the factory worker an honorary android, following proprietary algorithms around the giant warehouse like a remote-control shopping trolley. Amazon especially seems determined to midwife a new hybrid species, born of the cold and clinical romance between Fordist modularization and Taylorist maximization of efficiency. Every day, we hear more news reports detailing the distressing story of Amazon employees who have worked until they've collapsed, or who have continued to shovel cheap, toxic, plastic crap into boxes until their bladders have burst or their kidneys exploded

---

3   Heike Geissler, *Seasonal Associate* (Los Angeles: Semiotext(e), 2018).

for lack of humane bathroom breaks. No doubt Jeff Bezos is funding experiments charged with breeding a humanoid animal capable of working dexterously with polystyrene peanuts, for a wage *amounting* to peanuts, and without the traditional inconvenience of producing organic waste. (I believe the scientists will get a sizable bonus if this docile creature becomes hostile at the word "union.")[4] After all, as Taylor well understood, time is money.

Today, the line between the factory and other types of workplace is unclear. Your office may seem cool to the point of chill — with alt-pop music, beanbags, free cereal, and a foosball table — but in practice it is essentially a factory in hip clothing, in which employees churn out code or copy or "content" in one ephemeral form or another. Even something like the university — whose mission was to produce the type of people who don't have to worry about ever working in a factory — is now run on similar principles to Foxconn or Ford. Students are now the sausage we have been warned not to examine too closely.

One of the first things committed to celluloid was footage of workers from the Lumière Brothers' pioneering factory in Lyon leaving for home in 1895. By turning the camera on the building in which such cameras were being made — and on the people whose hands made them — this historic film became essentially a self-portrait of cinema itself, and of the labor that was to be so quickly effaced from the screen. Indeed,

---

4   In the meantime, a film like Alex Rivera's *Sleep Dealer* (2008) — set in the near future, when low-paid workers from third-world countries use virtual reality interfaces to work in factories still located in the developed world — presents the most likely (d)evolution of the economic paradigm.

it is remarkable that when the technology of cinema was itself only a year old, there was already a factory and a labor pool dedicated to shepherding this new art and medium through its infancy. A few decades later, in its golden age, Hollywood — across the pond — was regularly referred to as "the dream factory," suggesting that even our most intimate fancies and fantasies were now, in this brave new century, being engineered at an industrial scale and according to modern commercial techniques. In 2010, Andrew Norman Wilson filmed his own homage to the Lumière Brothers' primal scene, called *Workers Leaving the Googleplex*.[5] This clandestine effort depicted all the different levels of workers heading home — some branded with different colored badges denoting their lower place in the hierarchy, descending from executives, down to coders, all the way down to security guards and cleaners.

In sum, with the invention of moving pictures and digital computers, the logic of the factory now applies in every workplace, even as the factory itself comes to seem like a nineteenth-century relic to most people. And just as Jean Baudrillard insisted that Disneyland exists in order to make the rest of America seem real, we might also say that the factory persists today in order to convince us that we aren't *all* factory workers.

---

5   https://vimeo.com/15852288

The Tin Pusher

The "tin pusher" — or air-traffic controller — pays attention to the tiny dots moving about on his radar screen. Each dot represents a plane currently approaching an airport, which could contain up to eight hundred passengers (as in the case of the Airbus A380). In terms of sheer focus, we would be hard-pressed to find a more intense example of concentration. One microsecond of distraction can, in this instance, potentially lead to disaster and the loss of many lives. This adds not only a certain level of frisson to the job, but also an anonymous kind of heroism to those who safely usher us from one element (the ether) to the other (the earth). The tin pusher's superhuman capacity to focus on a single virtual world — the digital representation of the actual planes circling the runways — is in some ways quasi-divine (watching the world from above and making consequential, mortal decisions, often merely on a reflex), and in other ways profane and depraved (as detailed in the famous piece of reportage that formed the basis of the Hollywood film *Pushing Tin*).[1] In an article by Darcy Frey — which inspired the film, and which revolves around the charismatic controller Tom "Zack" Zaccheo — we learn about the white-knuckle grind of this larger-than-life console cowboy: a stereotypically vulgar, arrogant, and abrasive New

---

1   Darcy Frey, "Something's Got to Give," *New York Times*, March 24, 1996. https://www.nytimes.com/1996/03/24/magazine/something-s-got-to-give.html

Yorker, who flaunts his exceptional capacity to play a 3D game of Frogger with human souls traveling at six miles a minute.

In hair-raising detail, Frey describes "these controller-magicians" with "that savage, bug-eyed look, like men on the verge of drowning." Hunched over "banks of luminous radar scopes" and hopped up on caffeine and adrenaline, these men (and they are mostly men) are depicted as twitching like "a gathering of Tourette sufferers" as they try to juggle these metal balls in the air before easing them safely to the ground. The average professional life at the glowing interface is around four years, since there is, understandably, a high burnout rate given the intensity of focus — and the sheer force of gravity and mortality — that comes with the job. Zack, however, is a veteran, working his fourteenth year. He expresses a love-hate relationship with the pressure — he's addicted to the adrenaline, if not the coffee. Moreover, he gets a sick kick from the power. ("Pilots are like dogs," he says under his breath. "They can smell fear in your voice. But if you sound confident, they'll do whatever you tell them to do.")

Frey's article was written in 1996, just at the beginning of the home computer explosion and the first mass adoption of the Internet. Nevertheless, he had clearly frequented enough video game arcades in his time to make the analogy with a joystick jockey. (Today, of course, we live in a culture where autistic application to video game play can yield undreamed of fame, trophies, and prize winnings — at least for the especially nimble of wrist and focused of mind.) If we were seeking a more highbrow analogy, we would find one in the form of the symphonic conductor, using his baton to keep an entire orchestra aloft in suspended sonic animation. (Though we must also acknowledge that the conductor is often a figure that invites comic imitation, since his whole body is involved in the process. Such excessive physical exertion is amusing to a culture premised on gestural subtlety, or at least to those who have not yet learned to suppress their amusement at such excess.) In contrast to the conductor, the video gamer or tin pusher betrays very little physical motion. All his energy is concentrated in the synapses between his eyes, brain, reflexes, and nervous system. There is an economy to the lack of movement: minimal motion for maximal attention. Indeed, another air-traffic controller quoted in Frey's article, who goes by the less than reassuring nickname Jughead, explains that his video-game-like virtuosity relies on a certain mental disavowal (one which will have a much more sinister resonance in our own age of remote-controlled drone killings). "These aren't lives here," Jughead tells himself, pointing at the dots on the screen. "Otherwise, the stress is too much. You'd have a heart attack. You'd be done."

Today, it is apparent that the tin pusher is an early citizen of that addictive, nebulous sphere that Natasha Dow Schüll calls "the machine zone": a paradoxical space in which one's mind is both intensely present and focused, and also strangely diffused and relaxed. One might even call it a modern Zen state (although traditional Buddhists would rightly object to this popular misrepresentation, along with its conflation of mental clarity with a pulsing form of electrified hypnotism). In her already classic piece of cultural ethnography *Addiction by Design: Machine Gambling in Las Vegas,* Schüll interviews a casino patron called Mollie, who spends most of each day pressing buttons on the latest technical evolution of the old "one-armed bandit." Mollie explains:

> "The thing people never understand is that *I'm not playing to win.*"

Why, then, does she play? "To keep playing — to stay in that machine zone where nothing else matters."

I ask Mollie to describe the machine zone. She looks out the window at the colorful movement of lights, her fingers playing on the tabletop between us. "It's like being in the eye of a storm, is how I'd describe it. Your vision is clear on the machine in front of you but the whole world is spinning around you, and you can't really hear anything. You aren't really there — you're with the machine and that's all you're with."[2]

The analogy breaks down, however, when we remember that no lives are at stake — literally, immediately — when it comes to gambling machines. (Here the cost is measured in less-spectacular catastrophic potentialities. Although, if one were to actually tally up the body count of gambling-machine addiction, it would be significantly higher than that of plane crashes.) Even so, the cultural, gestural, and psychological fascia that connects these three figures — the marathon video gamer, the sleep-deprived video gambler, and the twitchy air-traffic controller — says much about the fate and future of human attentional resources and the way these are increasingly integrated into highly sophisticated, machinic networks. While it is true that we now have drones equipped with algorithms that can decide whether any given flickering figure caught in the digital crosshairs should live or die, we still rely on the human nervous system to oversee proceedings, if only as a vestigial witness or belated corrective. The tin pusher may display the balls and bravado of Tom Zaccheo,

---

2   Natasha Dow Schüll, *Addiction By Design: Gambling in Las Vegas* (Princeton, NJ: Princeton University Press, 2012), p.2.

but increasingly it seems the case that the "tin" itself is in fact pushing the likes of him.

At the height of summer, 1981, nearly 13,000 air-traffic controllers went on strike, forcing the complex Tetris of domestic and international air travel to a grinding halt. Their demands were for higher pay, shorter hours, and better equipment, since their own nerves had, for years, been obliged to make up for the daily failings of dangerously outdated technologies. Their paychecks did not, they maintained, reflect the relentless pressure that they were under: sweating and toiling in windowless transport offices akin to giant overheating microwaves; their own skulls — juggling dozens of airplanes at once, suspended in the virtual airspace of their own minds — likely to blow at any moment like an egg in a microwave. President Ronald Reagan, who had swept to power the year before on promises of tough-guy interventions (and who had, ironically, played a fighter pilot in several films), swiftly fired 11,359 air-traffic controllers after only two days of negotiations (even adding a stipulation that not a single one of them be rehired in the future, even if they recanted their blasphemous position in the cruel dawn of hardline neo-liberalism).

Pushing tin in our own time is, in line with the spirit of the age, less a question of macho swagger and competition, and more a matter of efficient anonymity. Which is not to say that the pressure falls any less heavily on the individuals who steer our planes safely down to the tarmac today. But the performance of attention is less flamboyant than it was before the turn of the millennium: less demonstrative, and presenting less of an occasion for even a nicotine-stained kind of glamor. Today, one is expected to punch in as one might at a telemarketer position, move pixelated units safely around the screen, and then clock off again. One is free to socialize with one's colleagues, of course, but any showy attempts to measure attention spans — as one might measure biceps or penises — should be left in the fetid locker room of the late twentieth century. The difference between the telemarketer and the tin pusher, however, is that the latter must pass a rigorous psychological test, designed to evaluate reliability and moral fiber. He must convince his bosses not only that he is *capable* of juggling thousands of lives in the air like so many ninepins, but also that he has each passenger's welfare at heart, and that he does not have any ideological reason for breaching the trust of those who employ him.

For there is something about the hubris of human flight that makes the collective effort to keep gravity at bay that much more potentially tragic, as in the story of Icarus. Flying above Nebraska, clutching a small plastic tub of reconstituted orange juice, may not feel heroic, but it may well — from the point of view of the jealous gods — be deemed, on a whim, to be flying too close to the sun. As Paul Virilio observed, once you invent the airplane, you simultaneously invent the plane crash.

Better to keep one's feet on the ground and pay attention to one's own trajectory. For then, a lapse in concentration — or even a flagrant abdication of attention — need not end so badly. Take for instance the veteran, decorated policeman — in Bangkok, I believe — who had safely directed traffic at one of the city's busiest crossroads for over two decades. Eventually, the logistics, momentum, and pressure just became too much for him (or perhaps it was simply boredom, as he had mastered the job so thoroughly). Without warning or notice, he blew his whistle constantly and freely — its piercing shriek suddenly liberated from any operational logic. And he danced about the junction, like a manic imp, among the ensuing chaos of his own creation.

The Massage Therapist

The massage therapist pays attention to the unique human geography of whatever body is laid out on the massage table before her. She kneads and pounds, pulls and stretches, chops and strokes, following the aching ley lines of the customer's form, tracing the skeleton, tenderizing the muscles, and quickening the nervous system. As such, the massage therapist represents a tactile form of attention that is usually only reserved for the lover (or sex worker). Indeed, it must be admitted that an ambiguous kind of "impersonal intimacy" is created by the massage process, which is why people often find them awkward or embarrassing. It is also why some of the seedier establishments — the downtown "massage parlors," for instance — sometimes cross the line between professional, therapeutic massage and a more libidinal form of relief (the infamous "happy ending"). Awareness of this line is crucial when it comes to the massage therapist, and it not only should *not* be crossed — like some kind of sleazy Rubicon — but it should not even be evoked in any sense as an elephant in the room, even in jest. For no matter what Deleuze and Guattari say, the body is a sensitive assemblage of *organs*, and can become confused concerning the distinction between the sexual and the sensual when it comes to modes of touch and caress if the mind does not attend to context, decorum, etiquette, respect, and so on. This is to say, the massage therapist is usually a pro when it comes to banishing the sexual in favor of the sensual, and they do this by removing themselves from the equation (while leaving the massage itself firmly intact). This is something like a tactful magic act or disappearing trick — a foregrounding of the act, and an effacing of the person doing the performance (like those puppeteers dressed head to toe in black so as not to distract the audience from their manipulations).

There are different forms and philosophies of massage, all designed to reorient the body in a very literal, hands-on way. The dominant ones advertised in trendy spas around the world today tend to be rooted in two broad traditions: the European (Swedish) technique, and the Asian (Chinese or Japanese) approach. Swedish massage is, unsurprisingly, a relatively pragmatic method: a kind of diagnostic seek-and-soothe system that finds knots and gnarls wherever they happen to have clustered, then breaks them down through applied pressure so that the healing blood can flow once again. In contrast, the Chinese medical massage — or the Japanese shiatsu which follows the same essential somatic maps — works on the principal of stimulating key points along the relevant meridians that correspond to the pain or blockages of the patient. The latter tends to be more holistic, though this can depend on the way the massage therapist deploys her strategic interventions.

The massage therapist can, depending on the experience of the patient-cum-customer, either be slandered as a sinner or praised as a saint (and indeed, the distinction between patient and customer — carried in the mind of the person paying for the treatment — can color one's interpretation of the effectiveness, or ineffectiveness, of the experience). This is to say, the massage therapist can be condemned as a charlatan, or even a pervert, if the massage is executed badly... or inappropriately. Or she can be described as a genius, a great diviner — even a lifesaver — if she affords the person, now flooded with endorphins, sweet relief from whatever ailment sent them to seek treatment in the first place. (In passing, we might compare the skills and sensitivities of the massage therapist with those of the DJ in terms of their shared, deep, empathic genius for manipulation, rhythm, and release. Certainly both vocations hold the potential to inspire others to bear witness to an almost miraculous capacity to bestow salvation precisely through an *explicitly embodied* attention ecology.)

The massage therapist must not only quickly assess the topology of the body — now splayed out on her massage table — in the manner of a civic quantity surveyor, but also summon a swift sense of the customer's overall affect and "sensibility" (meant in both senses of the term, referring to physiological response and mental-cultural orientation). She must ascertain not only what pressure and techniques to use, but also what tactile tricks might best bypass or outwit the psychological resistances that we carry around in our joints and tissues on a daily, accumulating basis. (For a massage therapist is well positioned to scorn the notion of a hard and fast body-mind distinction. She is anything but a Cartesian.)

The massage therapist is, in other words, a cross between doctor, detective, psychoanalyst, and lover (the three licensed professions working together to effectively neutralize the erotic essence of the remaining term, while keeping its inherently intimate mode of attention, its ability to closely "read" the body thus presented and to interpret the traces of its traumas — great and small — through a natural form of haptic hermeneutics). But just as a sizable percentage of people lack the pharmakon of physical love — no matter how much everyone "deserves" such human connection — only a certain tax bracket can regularly afford the special attentions of the massage therapist. (Imagine how much better the universal human mood would be if massage was open to more people!) Indeed, the massage therapist is a figure associated with wealth and luxury — something only the privileged minority can access. The massage therapist is thus but one foot soldier in the affluent person's private army, assembled to battle against the less dignified aspects of being human (an army comprised of cooks, cleaners, drivers, designers, planners, therapists, escorts, and so on). Which is all to say that we must not forget that the massage therapist's attention is a precious resource, and one that does not come cheap (a reminder which opens up to the wider point that *all* types of attention, when leased from another person, come with a cost, either in terms of money or via some other form of barter or exchange, whether explicitly signaled or not).

It's interesting to note, then, how rarely the massage therapist is depicted in popular culture, or even high culture, given how important she is to those who underwrite the culture industry. In films, for instance, she is usually a figure of (highly inappropriate) erotic fascination, or merely a mute plot device to render one of the main characters more vulnerable (since nudity complicates the credibility or competence of a protagonist). The massage therapist is not entirely trusted — perhaps a legacy of her adjacency to the lover (who, of course, is ever only a heartbeat away from double-crossing the one who covets her love). Her literal *manipulations* (the origin of the word is rooted in the Latin word for "handful") are, we suspect, too easily transferred into the register of psychology and impressionable behavior. Massage can be, from a certain angle, a physical form of hypnosis. And the essential oils and incense which so often accompany the ritual may indeed sometimes be deployed to mask a whiff of sulfur.

The massage therapist is expected to be skillful, intuitive, trustworthy, and discreet. It is even rumored that the massage therapists who work in the historic Russian Baths in New York's East Village are employed on account of their congenital deafness, since the gangsters who still frequent this less than luxurious spa are not overly endowed in the trust department.[1] One must, however, trust the massage therapist absolutely if planning to undress before them and literally put one's body in her hands. (While not technically a massage therapist, chiropractors use similar techniques, and have been known — on very rare occasions, it must be said — to tragically and suddenly end the lives of their patients.) In any case, we are at the massage therapist's mercy, and thus, structurally at least, she suddenly occupies the position of a god: a pagan divinity. The massage therapist thus retains traces of a heavenly lineage, forgiving us our primordial nudity, intervening in the knotted landscape of our fallen bodies, healing us with messianic charity, and allowing us to walk, dance, or play tennis again. Even if we pay her well, her art — when performed well — is experienced as a gift, since it returns us to something approximating the organic "factory setting" that forms the foundation of everything we do. It restores us to blessed functionality.

Does such language suggest a future in which we may have a kind of socialized access to an array of personal, automated massage therapists? Alas, this scenario seems unlikely given

---

1   Compare Japan's famous character Zatoichi — the protagonist of no less than twenty-six feature films — who is a nomadic, blind massage therapist and swordsman, able to intuit the good man from the bad, primarily through the sensitivity of his expert fingertips.

the fact that most robots have difficulty doing the most rudimentary activities mastered over millions of years by the human hand (thanks to its marvelous opposable thumb). Even if we could somehow perfectly engineer machines to mimic the movements of our fingers, they would not have the exquisite sympathetic-feedback systems required to adjust pressure accordingly and to respond in real time to the physiological, emotional — and even spiritual — needs of the patient. For the foreseeable future, at least, the massage therapist embodies a quintessentially mammalian form of attention — one shared by some other charismatic animals in their gentle caresses and grooming (and perhaps even by the critters deemed less charismatic, in ways we can't see, fathom, or understand). Indeed, from this angle, the massage therapist represents the civilized codification of our evolutionary urge to reach out and touch, to lower our defenses and be touched. As the philosopher might say: massage is a *medium* — part natural, part cultural — that helps facilitate inter-subjective communication.[2] Ritualized or formalized touch is the refined, "cooked" version of the raw human need and desire to be caressed, to be understood through touch. This is why the massage therapist is such an ambiguous figure: part intimate partner, part distant diagnostician. But in a modern world like ours, where we like our social demarcations to be clear and legible, the massage therapist is someone we can outsource certain intimacies to — with no strings attached, other than the ones that lead to our wallet — in order that we may be nimble enough to fight, or to love, another day.

---

2   Marshall McLuhan, *The Medium is the Massage* (London: Penguin, 1967).

The Monk

The monk pays attention to the spiritual solicitations of the world. But what might this mean, exactly? We could venture a response by pointing to the ways in which the Creator manifests the Holy Spirit in Creation, in the matter and manner of things. In paying attention to something deeper and more essential than what simply presents itself to our senses, however, the monk must withdraw from the world as much as possible. There is thus a deep contradiction in the ascetic life: a desire to decipher the sacred message that is both written within but also obscured by the fallen terrain of earthly existence. The monk retreats to the silence of the monastery, cave, or desert in order to better hear the voice of God, which is usually drowned out by the din of daily life. But this withdrawal from profane activity, and the dull buzzing it produces in the place of authentic thought, leads to yet another paradox, since the monk is now mostly left to his own devices. In other words, the monk must almost literally "get over himself" in order to find enlightenment, as he only really has himself for company. Monkish existence is thus an attempt to attend, with exceptional intensity, to the way in which the world not only "worlds" the self into Being, across the stretched thread of each day, but also unravels the rather pointless contingency of individuality. Prayer — as a concentrated, global technology of devout attention — thus uses the self to *transcend* the self, and to at least begin the long journey of understanding the profound interconnection of All That Is.

We must be careful, however, not to mix up traditions, even as we may see some fundamental universals linking them across ages and continents. Buddhist monks, for instance, are more likely to emphasize the karmic continuity of souls through time — human and animal alike — as if the universe were a giant launderette and our selves so many (temporarily) lost socks. Christian monks, however, are more likely to meditate on the temptations of the flesh and the ways in which this short journey through the rather sordid Valley of Life is but a forsaken way station before the grace, or damnation, of Eternity. Within this particular cosmology, our own earthly guise is considered but a dress rehearsal for eternal singularity. And whether this is to be enjoyed in the refreshing celestial country club of heaven or endured in the overheated La Guardia–style waiting gates of hell is up to us and our conscience (vis-à-vis Christ, the shepherd of souls).

Such relentless attention to the surreal, liminal plight of mortality — whether practiced in the West or the East — is no picnic, however. And monks bear a heavy burden in focusing on the Eternal that lies buried in the heart of every moment like a dormant seed. The human mind is not built to be a mirror of God, for it fogs up easily. It fractures and mottles. And it is no coincidence that the Bible notes that we tend to only see truly "through a glass darkly." No doubt this is why monks have historically been especially susceptible to *acedia*, a specific species of low spirits not quite captured by more familiar names such as depression, listlessness, or melancholy. Known also as "the noonday demon," acedia can be the fruit of excessive attention to things beyond human ken or control. When dwelling night and day with, and within, the divine, the monk may understandably suffer from feelings of inadequacy, insecurity — even superfluity. "What's the point?" asks the monk in his heart of hearts, having already consulted illuminated manuscripts, or the curve of a tree trunk, for an answer but come up wanting.

As the philosopher Giorgio Agamben explains, acedia combines sloth, sorrow, and *taedium vitae* (the weariness of life). It is what can happen when the exhortation to attention is pushed to its limits and then collapses in on itself. Where the monk sought stillness, clarity, and illumination, he finds instead *evagatio mentis*, or the wandering mind: "the petulant incapability of fixing an order and a rhythm to one's own thought."[1] Whether tortured by visions of lust spawned in the clammy cells of celibacy, or dragged down by the seemingly sourceless lethargy of ennui, the monk is forced, by the nature of his calling, to pay strict and consistent heed to the bankruptcy of his own attentional capacity.

Again, different traditions have distinct strategies for dealing with the exceptionalism of monkish concerns and the various techniques they have developed over centuries to refine them. These, in turn, tend to branch off into the severe or the voluptuous (both efficient routes to the ecstatic). Catholics, for instance, have offered self-flagellation with one hand, and the contemplative cultivation of rose gardens with the other. Hindu mystics have chosen between sleeping on a bed of nails and indulging in fragrant Tantric exertions. Buddhist monks have, depending on the region and the

---

1   Giorgio Agamben, *Stanzas: Word and Phantasm in Western Culture* (Minneapolis: University of Minnesota Press, 1993), p. 5.

period, opted between insomniac meditation and well-nourished concerts. Whereas for the devout Sufi, grace can be achieved either by fasting or by dancing and whirling into a consecrated bliss.[2] The monk is thus a figure of profane inversion: an animated fragment of the fallen world that seeks to project himself into a sacral state through the will of a divine aspiration.

Consider the parable of the fifteenth-century Zen monk Ikkyu:

> One day a man of the people said to Zen Master Ikkyu: "Master, will you please write for me some maxims of the highest wisdom?"
>
> Ikkyu immediately took his brush and wrote the word "Attention."
>
> "Is that all?" asked the man. "Will you not add something more?"
>
> Ikkyu then wrote twice running: "Attention. Attention."
>
> "Well," remarked the man rather irritably, "I really don't see much depth or subtlety in what you have just written."
>
> Then Ikkyu wrote the same word three times running: "Attention. Attention. Attention."
>
> Half-angered, the man demanded: "What does that word 'attention' mean anyway?"

---

2   "The Sufi's night is the day of ordinary men," writes Haytham El Wardany, in his *Book of Sleep*, "and his absence is their presence. In absence, a person is present between the hands of his lord, heedful and attentive; in waking, he returns to the created world around him and forgets Truth."

And Ikkyu answered gently: "Attention means attention."[3]

The Zen master here seems to be drawing attention to the self-evident wisdom of attention itself, as if to suggest that, rather than turtles, it's this faculty, or orientation, that upholds the world, "all the way down." Attention is presented as an argument made convincingly, albeit tautologically, in a single word. But even if the devotee grasps the import or deeper resonance of the koan as framed by the master, the question still remains: To *what* are we supposed to attend? Should we be paying closer heed to the world itself, in order to better see the fingerprint of God? Or should we shut our eyes to the trivial shifting of things, to see *through* the mere appearance of existence and into its deeper reality? (An ageless theme, directly connecting Plato's cave to *The Matrix*.)

Ikkyu himself was not your typical Zen monk, shut away in his monastery inhaling incense and nibbling modestly on whatever meager fare the local villagers would donate in exchange for a blessing. He liked to drink sake, to speak back to his masters, and to pinch the plump pork buns of the local ladies. He was a musician and master calligrapher, who is said to have introduced the ceremonial approach to drinking a cup of tea. From these biographical tidbits it is clear that Ikkyu preferred to offer his prayers through the medium of the world itself, believing enlightenment to be less a glowing, golden carrot, suspended beyond the horizon, than a prostitute's red lantern, flickering outside an *onsen*.

---

3   Philip Kapleau, *The Three Pillars of Zen: Teaching, Practice, and Enlightenment* (New York: Anchor Books, 1980).

Attending carefully to what *is* — with one's full spirit, and with the plenitude of senses — may be the most reliable way to truly apprehend what *was* and always *will be*. The classic distinction between the material and the spiritual turns out to be a ruse. While diving into the messy flux of life may *appear* to be the least intuitive way for a monastic soul to live a spiritual life, even Dionysus himself could — from an admittedly perverse angle — be portrayed as an ascetic by way of excess. The monk seeks to either subtract the world and be left with its essence, or to enhance its presence and to bask in its aura. Whichever strategy is eventually deployed in earnest, attention is the divine channel which must be vigilantly (or ecstatically) opened in order to experience the Godhead. For enlightenment needs the right wiring, so to speak, in order to conduct itself to our consciousness, just as surely as a tungsten lightbulb needs copper filaments to conduct electricity.

How many monks does it take to change a lightbulb?

Only Ikkyu really knows.

"Attention."

The Surfer

The surfer pays attention to the fluxing undulations of the ocean. In doing so, her attention is not taken up with a single object (*the* ocean), but with the specific way — sometimes chaotic, sometimes highly patterned — in which this great element refracts into a series of approaching waves, each distinct from the last. At a glance from the sand, the experienced surfer can glean a good sense of the tide, current, swell, and overall mood of Neptune's playground. It is not until she is in the sea itself, however, that she is really immersed in the liquid grain of the water, which can change at any moment. The surfer instinctively understands Heraclitus's famous statement — that one can never step into the same stream twice. In her case, however, she lives this flowing truism with the infinitely more complex dynamics of the sea. The surfer thus watches the surface — sometimes churning, other times as smooth as glass — with the intense focus of a child, forever hopeful that the mood of Mother Ocean will be in harmony with the serious business of the day: play.

We might even go so far as to say that the surfer turns the sober act of land surveying into a sport by adapting every cell of her body — every fiber of her being — to the far more treacherous topography of water. Here she guides her beloved surfboard — at such times an extension of herself — to glide over "the lay of the land." In this altogether more challenging element, in which any given angle or orientation lasts a split second, she is in a heightened state of awareness, anticipating the shapes and curves to come. (The skateboarder, by contrast — in an unconscious homage to the arc of evolution — brings the board on to terra firma, adds some wheels, and then "surfs" the frozen waves of concrete and steel.)

Beyond the immediacy of the oncoming breakers, the surfer must also clock the overall environment, including the weather (especially any approaching storms that might whip up the tide), other surfers (particularly any aggressive or inexperienced interlopers), and other potentially hazardous elements (such as submerged rocks or coral). The main motivation, however, for leaving the security of the shore and paddling out toward the surf is to open oneself up to that almost religious feeling when things go well.[1] At such times, the surfer controls the wave like a rodeo champion. But at the same time, she suddenly feels completely at one with its curling, surging intensity. In the midst of the perfect ride — or even during a few seconds of an imperfect one — the surfer thus simultaneously dominates and melts into the infinite, dissolving power of the ocean. It is a sensation at once clarifying and absolving, reinforcing and releasing, transcendent and deeply imminent. And it is one of the most addictive sensations one can experience (hence those circulating tales of successful business people who, after getting a taste of the surfing life, give up everything to chase the perfect wave for

---

1   The quintessential surf movie, *The Endless Summer* (1965) documents the pilgrimage of a group of wave-chasers who follow the warm weather around the globe. A running joke throughout the film is that our sun-kissed searchers are told over and over again, at famous beaches on different continents, that "they should have been here yesterday."

the rest of their lives).[2] The surfer is thus yet another one of our paradoxical figures: both highly focused (only the wave really matters) and highly distracted (since 99.99 percent of her life is spent dealing with things that are, alas, *not* the perfect wave, and which are thus difficult to really commit to).

For our purposes, the surfer can be contrasted with the tracker, who builds up a picture in her mind of recent events by paying careful attention to the indexical traces in the environment (those being actual impressions, marks, or traces of previous entities or events, such as footprints in the snow or bullet holes in a wall). The tracker can therefore identify and reconstruct significant passages through the fourth dimension (that is, time), and the way these specific strands, or notable threads, weave their way through the three dimensions of space. (For instance, a tracker might say: "A wombat came through this part of the bush this morning, since these droppings are cube shaped and not yet dry.") The surfer, however, is not concerned with anything but the present moment. Even the previous wave, that passed by a matter of seconds ago, is expunged swiftly from consciousness as she scans the horizon for gathering signs of the next one. The tracker, like the detective, can reconstruct the past in order to make decisions or judgments in the present, mindful of tomorrow. The surfer, by contrast, is suspended in

2   It would not be an exaggeration to talk of an *erotics* of surfing, even as it seems surreal to assume an intimacy with something as vast as the ocean. Here, we might better apply the Lacanian notion of "extimacy," whereby we find ourselves profoundly impacted by abstract, impersonal, and alien forces arriving from outside, from elsewhere (and which are thus unassimilable to conventional, sentimental narratives of love, or romantic fusion).

the here and now, as the vectors of undulating actuality lift her up into the rolling foam of the immediate future. (Like a melody, the attention of the surfer is implicated in Henri Bergson's key notion of *durée* — a term coined to describe that philosopher's belief that time flows organically, and smoothly, from one state to the other, rather than stochastically passing an invisible baton between a temporally distinct past, present, then future.)[3] Time, for the surfer, washes around her body, rippling outward. It does not pass by in linear fashion (or if it does, the linearity is itself tubular). The only time the present is rather violently ruptured by the future is when the surfer is unceremoniously dumped deep beneath the churning surface of the water. Then her whole being goes into emergency mode, concentrating on the task of holding her breath for as long as it takes to resurface safely. The exhilaration of sparring with such a formidable opponent means that the surfer is surfing as much on adrenaline as on salt water.

Beyond the metaphysics of the thing, the surfer is a sociological, even an anthropological type. She tends to represent a certain subculture, aesthetic, or lifestyle: the beach bum, the hippie, the dude or dudette. As such, she tends to favor the organic, the counter-cultural, the THC infused, and the patchouli scented (or at least that's the popular stereotype). Her hair is dreadlocked from the salt, her clothes utilitarian and unpretentious, and her feet prefer to be unshod. When

---

3   To a quantum physicist, we may all be considered "surfers" in one form or another, even if we never dip our toe in the ocean. This is due to the fact that this mind-bending theory of things posits existence (and existents) as less a collection of objects within space and moving through time than an almost infinitely large wave function, rolling through (and simultaneously *creating*) the Real.

not actively surfing, she is waxing her board, talking to other surfers about undiscovered beaches, and thinking about how she can continue to tweak her life to maximize the chance of finding the perfect wave. Her attention ecology is thus an idealized alternative to the daily grind — a utopian option for those looking to opt out of the rat race. (We all, at some point, dream of "dropping out" and trying our luck with the oceanic gods, perhaps unconsciously inspired by watching Gidget movies or *The Teenage Mutant Ninja Turtles* as children: "Cowabunga, dude!")

The surfer is the very embodiment of the optimist, since no matter how crappy the conditions, the perfect wave still beckons, elsewhere or elsewhen, and she will do almost anything to keep chasing it. Surfing is thus a wholesome form of addiction, with no harmful side effects to really speak of except minor rashes, ear infections, sunburn, and the very occasional shark bite.[4] The surfer comes closer than most to being in harmony with the elements and their natural frequencies. And when she closes her eyes at night, she can still see, and feel, the swell approaching her, lifting her up, and laying her down. (Perhaps even her own somatic cycle is synchronized with the phases of the moon, which in turn directly affect the size and rhythm of the tides.)

It is amusing, then, to look back on the mid-1990s, when everyone was excited about "surfing the web" (and so distracted by chat rooms and pixelated skin that we didn't even notice the strange mixed metaphor). Through the force of analogy, the Internet was presented as a vast

---

4   Drownings are surprisingly infrequent given how many people challenge Neptune to a friendly duel on any given day, even in places as unlikely as Cornwall or Lake Michigan.

ocean of information through which anyone with a modem could paddle and surf at will and according to their whim. (Indeed, one of the first Internet browsers was called Netscape Navigator, and branded itself with the logo of a ship's wheel.) And while it's true that the first few years of being online could provide moments of serotonin, or even adrenaline — via the futuristic novelty of communicating with people in real time on the other side of the world — this type of "surfing" would, over time, deliver diminishing returns and lose its aquatic associations altogether. Still suggestive, however, is the fact that these two types of surfing are strongly connected in the popular mind with the idea of the California dream, where a successful Silicon Valley CEO can take a meeting, barefoot on his Instagrammable verandah, and then surf the waves in his state-of-the-art wetsuit, before driving in his sportscar to a business lunch in Santa Cruz.[5] (As Don DeLillo put it so well, "Californians invented the idea of 'lifestyle.' And this alone warrants their doom.")[6]

The enduring appeal of surfing itself — or of the figure of the surfer in popular culture — has its roots in the aforementioned quasi-religious aspect of the practice. Surfing is alluring precisely because it does not leave anything in its wake; it does not *produce* anything (other than euphoria,

---

5   In Richard Barbrook and Andy Cameron's now classic essay "The Californian Ideology," the authors trace the way in which the radical West Coast counterculture of the 1960s quickly became depoliticized in the 1970s and '80s and rendered into simple aesthetic and aspirational "boho" tropes of New Age–inflected "dot.com neoliberalism." https://www.metamute.org/editorial/articles/californian-ideology

6   Don DeLillo, *White Noise* (New York: Penguin, 2016), p. 66.

on a good day, or the determination to do better next time when the elements conspire against the surfer). In his attempt to describe the indescribable, Immanuel Kant resorted to the experience one might have when facing a giant, looming mountain in the Alps. The sublime, he argued, refuses to be put into words; we can only *feel* it, in our own impotent insignificance. We can only point to it "offstage," as it were, or point to the extraordinary things (usually natural or artistic) that evoke a sense of the sublime in us while not exactly embodying it (for the sublime *sublimates* itself as we try to approach or grab hold. It evaporates into the unaccountable ether of the numinous). One wonders what Kant would have made of surfing had such a pastime been invented in his time. After all, the surfer is uniquely concerned with getting as close as she can to the sublime. Indeed, she is granted a special proximity to it by virtue of her renunciation of the desire to *grasp* it, to clutch it close. Rather, she is content to simply ride along with it for the fleeting duration of a wave, vibing with its primal momentum as it dances toward the shore, gliding on the cusp of collapse and dissolution.

To see those enormous waves off the coast of Hawaii as a tropical storm approaches — to watch the surfer ride that fine line between living life to the fullest and surrendering to the death drive — is to feel an inkling of the lurching vertigo of the sublime.[7] To stand on the shore and witness these foolish,

---

7   From the perspective of the sublime, we might even consider Stanislaw Lem's masterpiece, *Solaris*, to be a highbrow "surfing" of the speculative implications of encountering a truly alien, sentient ocean. On the other end of the science fiction spectrum, we should also mention John Carpenter's comic, low-budget cult movie *Dark Star* (1974), in which one of the crew members of an exploded

courageous souls is to stand, like Kant, in front of a monstrous mountain. On this occasion, however, the mountain is now, unaccountably, rushing toward us. To be the surfer herself, however, riding the giant cliff face of crystal, is to pay profound attention to every micro-moment that separates ecstasy and agony. And yet, she is so involved in the moment that the experience feels less like a triumph or accomplishment than an absolute release or letting go — mentally, spiritually — even as every muscle tenses in the white-knuckle struggle against catastrophe. When she finally finds, and rides, the perfect wave, the surfer is no longer registering the world in the quotidian currency of attention. For she is — for those few eternal seconds — of a piece (and at peace) with the world itself, so deeply and fully *present* that there is no longer any distance or space of reflection from which to measure the quality or span of attention at all.

---

spaceship comes across a piece of asteroid shaped like a surfboard and hangs ten toward the atmosphere of a nearby planet, where he will surely combust like a falling star (a motif repeated in the climax of Kathryn Bigelow's popular 1991 movie *Point Break*, in which the main villain — a renegade surfer and bank robber known as Bodhi — rides the last, perfect wave of his life, since the swells at Bells Beach are, on that occasion, simply *too* sublime to survive).

The Dog

And what of the dog? What does she pay attention to?[1]

---

1   Certainly it would be extremely presumptuous to assume that I understand the lures, sparks, and triggers of the canine attention economy. I can, however, be reasonably confident in making claims regarding *what* interests a dog, simply through a lifetime of observation (even if I can't take the next step and explain *why*, or for what purpose — and according to which dictates — this interest asserts itself). It is well established, for instance, that dogs — considered collectively, as a species — are transfixed by objects that they can fetch: the classic example being the stick (large enough for some heft, but small enough to be tossed around by the dog's human companion). One might already object, however, that *wild* dogs, to whom our domestic pooch is distantly related, show little to no interest in such frivolous games. Moreover, many dogs of a more laconic or jaded disposition similarly betray a profound indifference, or even a pronounced aversion, to the whole fetch entertainment complex. In other words, just as it is a mistake — or at least an overgeneralization — to say that humans are interested in X or Y (where, say, X = money, or Y = sex), we make a similarly compromised claim when we suggest that *all* dogs love tummy rubs, or walkies, or sausages. Nevertheless, we must also concede that many dogs, if not most, enjoy some combination of these (just as many, if not most, humans are partial to money and sex — asceticism and headaches notwithstanding). Exceptions may or may not prove the rule. But we are obliged to traffic in generalities

Certainly she spends much of her time paying close olfactory attention to her environment. Whether leashed on city streets or intoxicatingly free in a forest, the dog sniffs and smells all sorts of tracks and traces that we can barely fathom, in both a sensual and an intellectual sense. The world "looks" completely different to the dog, because she is primarily looking through her nose. She therefore pays most attention to that which excites any given combination of the sensitive nerve endings in her nostrils. In the city, the dog seems to take very close note of saplings and fire hydrants, often pausing to leave some golden note or record of her own. Presumably this is a more sophisticated, animal equivalent of the graffiti that traditionally asserts, just for the ontological record, "Bobby woz 'ere." Then again, each ammonium-infused signature may contain more information that we can imagine. Such rich data streams may include the informational equivalent of a tweet, or even of the entire Sunday supplement. And in this way, the next dog to come along inhales the canine news of the day.

Indubitably, the dog pays attention to other dogs, either through enthusiastic lunging, hostile barking, or an exaggerated pose of disinterest. Humans, of course, register on her radar, but not with the vivid presence afforded by whatever pungent knowledge is conveyed through the sniffing of a fellow dog's butt. The dog notices squirrels, cats, and other smallish mammals to the degree that she enjoys having an excuse to indulge in the chase — her genetic legacy. The dog is, of course, vulnerable to training and conditioning. We only

---

if we want to think through a question. And in any case, it is worth at least briefly speculating about the ways in which the dog pays attention, if only to remind ourselves that we are not the only species blessed with this capacity.

know the name Pavlov ourselves because we were conditioned through the pedagogical context of his famous experiment, in which dogs learned to salivate at the sound of a bell even in the absence of promised nourishment or satisfaction (a lesson the advertising industry took close notice of, and which it has been exploiting with increasing nuance ever since). The dog can be trained — either deliberately or simply through the semiotics of routine — to seek out specific objects or gestures. The human putting on his boots, for instance, signifies an impending walk, triggering the accompanying excitement of anticipation in the canine mind and body. In the same manner, the human opening the kitchen drawer signals the search for a can opener, which in turn indicates the imminent enjoyment of food. Likewise, on the less pleasant end of the spectrum, the dog may hear the jingling of car keys and know she is about to be abandoned (whether for the workday or for the rest of her life, she can never be sure; though she seems to assume the latter, either as an emotional defense mechanism or a general disposition toward pessimistic fatalism).

The dog, in other words, pays constant and vigilant attention to the human who feeds her and who provides the most regular source of companionship. She is exquisitely attuned to his moods, his movements, and his whereabouts, just as she is hyper-aware of his attempts to communicate across the species barrier — his vocal tones, his gestures, his commands, his cajolements, his encouragements. The dog recognizes her name, even if this does not come with the same burden of identity that we ourselves bear. Nevertheless, she understands when she is being admonished, in sharp contrast to when she is being praised. (We can only speculate whether the dog notices that when she has transgressed the rules of the human world, she is reduced to her phylum — "bad dog!" — and that when she has upheld the values of her so-called owner, she is lifted up into the gendered universe — "good girl!")

Some believe that the dog is a little *too* good at reading human social cues and has betrayed her own, more feral nature in the process. The French philosopher Gilles Deleuze, for instance, described the dog as an Oedipal animal in order to convey the extent to which she becomes an honorary family member, now baggaged with all the neurotic symptoms and emotional blackmail this entails. For this reason, Deleuze went on to say that "barking is the stupidest sound in Nature." Why so? Because it is the sound of a once wild animal now flagrantly engaging in the indignity of trying to communicate her complaints in the human tongue, but without the proper vocal equipment. In any case, the dog is certainly suspended between her own instinctual interests and the regime installed by her human stewards. As a puppy, for instance, she has her nose rubbed in urine in an attempt to teach her the sin of relieving herself inside the home. She must learn, in other words, the violent lesson of the super-ego and develop an internalized conscience.

Other thinkers, however, believe that Deleuze's account romanticizes the wild animal to a dubious degree and does not allow for the creaturely companionship — the back-and-forth between two sensitive and sentient beings — that such cohabitation allows. Donna Haraway, especially, pays special attention to the intimate relationship that she has with her own "companion species": an Australian Shepherd called Cayenne. She insists that interspecies relationships have been messy, complicated, and contingent since the very beginning, and that we should not be tempted to draw such a sharp dividing line between nature and culture, wild and tame. Indeed, she goes to great lengths to avoid the kind of thinking that squares off one figure (the human) from another (the animal) and only then extracts some kind of ethical, or even ontological, lesson from the encounter. Rather, she sees animal-human relations as entangled, symbiotic, pragmatic, opportunistic, and mutually contaminating — and as thus all the more fascinating for it.[2] ("Dogs," she writes, "in their historical complexity...are not an alibi for other themes; dogs are fleshly material-semiotic presences.... Dogs are not surrogates for theory; they are not here just to think with. They are here to live with. Partners in the crime of human evolution.")[3]

Whether we incline more toward Deleuze's perspective or Haraway's, we can agree that the dog is an accomplished semiotician in many ways, one who can navigate all sorts of different environments and situations, and who can do an impressive job of moving between the natural and cultural worlds. (In this respect, she is a kind of shaggy amphibian.) Dogs can warn us about dangers we have yet to sense, and thus can be shepherds of our own attention. They can sniff out drugs or escaped convicts. (Deleuze will also note that the dog is much closer to being a cop than a cat ever will be.)[4] However, they can also guide the unsighted through densely

---

2   For an exceptionally moving portrait of just such a messy relationship, see Kelly Reichardt's 2008 film *Wendy and Lucy*.

3   Donna Haraway, *The Companion Species Manifesto* (Chicago: Prickly Paradigm Press, 2003), p. 5.

4   The attention of a cat is famously fickle, to the extent that people tend to be exceedingly grateful when their feline housemate pays them any mind beyond the purely transactional, communicational gestures that equate to "Feed me; I'm hungry," and "Clean the litterbox; it smells."

trafficked city streets, and sniff out diseases more efficiently than the most expensive and cutting-edge technology.

When all is said and done, the dog — through her tail-wagging, tongue-lagging, head-cocked attention — reminds us that the capacity to "take heed" or "dwell with" or "be present for" is not simply an individual capacity or facility, but also a relation: a negotiation between beings. Hence the emphasis on economy: sharing, trading, bartering, exchanging, investing, and so on. The dog pays attention to a universe of chemical messages that are invisible to us, while also — mostly! — respecting our mystifying exhortations (not to eat the toilet paper, not to get up on the couch, not to foil the daily hostile incursion of the postal carrier).

If attention is the greatest gift, as Simone Weil suggested, then dogs are a gift to humans, offered by another kind of being altogether. To feel "seen" is to be existentially (re)validated. And many people legitimately prefer the recognition of their dog to that of their teacher, priest, or colleague. For there is something more "pure" about the attention paid by a presence who does not know how to be duplicitous or disingenuous. The love of a dog has a very clear and straightforward price: affectionate petting, encouraging sounds, regular excursions, and the cost of a can of dog food.

The Ball Boy

The ball boy pays attention to the tennis ball as it bounces around the court, to the exclusion of everything else.[1] His entire person, in fact, is focused on the physics of the ball and its rubbery journey over and around the net. Indeed, the ball boy has been trained to such a pitch of perfection that he would presumably be hard-pressed to notice if every spectator at Wimbledon were suddenly to throw off their clothes and toss them on to the umpire's chair. Even such preposterous eccentricities as this would be of a second order of being for the ball boy, since, to him, the only object that enjoys full phenomenological favor is the ball itself (or rather, *balls* plural, since the typical professional tennis fixture uses over a hundred different ones during the course of the match). Of course, any given *individual* ball boy may indeed find himself distracted by something or other: a pesky pigeon, a bright red dress, a charismatic sports idol. But this would be a regrettable lapse in his focusing capacity — an exception that proves the rule. The *quintessential* ball boy has had his perceptual apparatus attuned and calibrated to such an extent that nothing exists in his world — in his hyper-specific *Umwelt* — other than the fuzzy yellow-green sphere that also comprises his raison

---

1   While it is true that at least half of the world's ball boys are girls these days, the name has stuck enough for me to use it here. The alternative, "ball kids," is too infantilizing, and "ball persons" is too formal and awkward.

d'être (to recklessly mix our German with our French). In this sense, the ball boy is akin to the dog, practically hypnotized by a game of fetch: absolutely fixated on the ball, charged with the sole mission of recovering the object and returning it from whence it came. The very fiber of the ball boy's being has been "taught to be taut." It has been pulled tight, like a violin bow, quivering on the point of breaking, but remaining coiled — a bundle of sheer potential energy — until the ball slams into the net or bounces off the sponsorship sign and the point has been decided. Then, and only then, does the ball boy spring into action, like a human whippet.

The ball boy is thus an instance of human attention, cultivated to a point of maximal intensity, starting to possess a practically creatural quality — becoming a matter of secondary instinct. Moving, for just a moment, down the evolutionary ladder, we may even note the similarity between the ball boy and the tick; the latter famously triggered into action — out from a deep and dormant sleep — by a single chemical catalyst (specifically, the presence of butyric acid, which itself signals the presence of a delicious mammal in the vicinity). The ball boy is tick-like in terms of his monomaniacal focus, but also dog-like in terms of the conditioning that he has undergone. (Consider, for instance, those popular YouTube videos in which a dog owner proudly displays his own pet's restraint by having it resist a doggy treat placed cruelly on its own nose. Only when given the correct signal is the poor pooch allowed to finally obey the clamor of his appetite and chow down. We might now imagine making the same kind of video, but instead featuring a hapless ball boy repressing his specific, newly disciplined instincts with great and visible effort while balancing a tennis ball on the bridge of his nose.)

Here, it might be worth pausing to note how the plight of the ball boy demonstrates the extent to which the general attention economy is driven by an implicit hierarchy. The higher a person sits on the social ladder, the more things they are *allowed* to pay attention to. The affluent, dilettante Renaissance man, for instance, is free to read the newspaper, survey the garden, bet on the horses, and conduct a love affair, all within a single afternoon; while, in sharp contrast, a factory worker in the same city is obliged to watch a single machine perform its monotonous function a thousand times an hour. Having made such a claim, however, it must also be admitted that the reverse can also be just as true: the less status and privilege one enjoys, the *higher* the number of things one is obliged to pay attention to (as any single parent struggling to hold down multiple jobs can confirm).

In any case, the ball boy might feasibly be considered the lowest of the low from the perspective of his impoverished attention ecology. For even an eighteenth-century slave tasked with fanning an emperor has the liberty to daydream of whatever he likes provided the fan keeps moving up and down in a regular rhythm. The ball boy, however, enjoys no such luxury, as his mind is just as shackled to the mandate of his service as his body. As such, the ball boy represents a kind of historical hangover from, or anachronistic throwback to, the days of overt, exotic, ceremonial service. Observe how he stands stiffly to attention at the beginning of each point, with the discipline of a mute and lowly courtier or palace guardian. There is something almost Egyptian about the abject excess with which the ball boy's entire person is dedicated to something as frivolous as a tennis ball, as if the ball itself outranked him. Indeed, it is as if the ball boy has been charged with ensuring an important ritual is performed smoothly, but on no account is he to catch the eye, or even be caught observing, the participants of the ritual itself. He is reduced to pure function — the infinite richness of his perceptual faculties compressed to a single, highly kinetic dot. To see the enthusiasm with which the ball boy scampers after a loose ball — or to witness the sheer servility with which he holds up a captured ball (a signal to the nearest gladiator that he is ready to help the game proceed) — is to notice that the ball boy seems to perversely enjoy his simplified programming, his own personal *reductio ad absurdum* — to the extent that he is most likely salivating a little at the prospect of fulfilling his demeaning duty. (One is therefore further forced to speculate: Will we replace the ball boy with efficient robots when the latter are dexterous enough? Or will we postpone this particular instance of obsolescence since we somehow prefer to watch the next generation acting like human Roombas?)

But what of the linesman? Isn't he similarly impoverished in terms of his attentional triggers (or similarly augmented, depended on the value you place in the human infrastructure of the game of tennis)? True, he shares with the ball boy a frightening, single-minded focus. In fact, he is even more laser targeted than the ball boy, since he is trained to ignore even the ball *except* for the moment when it enters his vision. No matter how exciting the play, he must watch the integrity of the white line with the unnerving attention of a lunatic and the unerring diligence of a long-haul trucker. In this sense, the linesman should be placed lower in the pecking order. But before we are tempted to demote the poor fellow, we must remember that his attention comes with a modicum of consequential authority: the judging of whether a ball is in or out. (And again, we might suspect that we only keep this

"human element" in the age of high-tech ball tracking in order
to make people do inhuman things.)

Indeed, the infrastructure of the game is a giant machinic
witness: a kind of deific panopticon, each element — each
and every ball boy and linesman — representing different
perspectives of some kind of distributed, all-seeing tennis God
(represented *in toto* by the umpire, of course, sitting up in the
sporting heavens on his ludicrous, man-baby high chair). This
all-seeing God, moreover, watches over the titans who play
the game, and who treat the ball boys like scuttling servants,
to be seen and not heard — and to be occasionally abused and
humiliated if the player is frustrated and needs a dog to kick.
(Ironic then, that some of the most legendary giants of tennis
began as ball boys, including Roger Federer, who once upon a
time scampered hither and thither around the courts in Basel
as a sprightly lad of twelve.)

In short, the ball boy tells us much about the extent to
which younger humans especially can be disciplined to learn
a kind of joy in bracketing out the overwhelming and almost
infinite stimuli of the world in order to prioritize a single
object or line. And while this type and intensity of attention
can only be expected to last the amount of time it takes to play
a few sets of tennis — and, even then, with plenty of breaks
to relax the attention muscles — it also lays bare the ambient
and semi-conscious sadistic pleasures of making other people
pay attention to only a tiny fragment of the picture while we
ourselves can enjoy the whole panorama.

The Surveillance Camera

The surveillance camera pays attention to everything that crosses its lens, since it registers the scene it is streaming or recording. Few would argue, however, that it is capable of paying any genuine attention given it has no mind or brain to process what it is witnessing. On the other hand, we should not be too hasty to dismiss this possibility in an age of sophisticated new software, algorithms, and machine learning. Many surveillance cameras are now programmed to read and "recognize" certain faces and certain expressions, alerting authorities if they spy a known fugitive or detect an agitated visage, suggesting nefarious intentions. Certainly, this form of attention is highly speculative and overcoded by ideological biases, to the extent that some have dubbed it little more than a new form of phrenology.[1] It is also wildly erratic and unreliable, routinely flagging innocent people as suspect. Why? Because the very presence of an all-seeing network of electronic eyes helps create the climate wherein people are — to quote the thinker most associated with the idea of the panopticon — "docile and useful."[2] People are more likely

---

1   Alex Najibi, "Racial Discrimination in Face Recognition Technology," *Science in the News*, Harvard, October 24, 2020. https://sitn.hms.harvard.edu/flash/2020/racial-discrimination-in-face-recognition-technology/

2   Michel Foucault, "Panopticism," *Discipline and Punish: The Birth of the Prison* (New York: Pantheon, 1977).

to act like sheep if they think their every movement is being watched by sheepdogs in uniform. When Jeremy Bentham proposed the panopticon as the perfect prison — since it is equally effective whether manned or not — he was simply secularizing the omnipresent efficiency of an all-seeing (and all-judging) God. Monotheistic religions draw much of their power and authority from the idea that no sin or transgression goes unwitnessed, and that thus all must be atoned for, one way or another. The "recording angel" — who chronicles every single event of every single life, no matter how fleeting or modest — flutters his snooping wings around the intrusive presence of the surveillance camera.

According to the wits of the Internet, there is an important mediating figure that sits between the ever-watchful divinity and the permanently alert security camera: the traditional Italian grandmother, for she spends the warm afternoons on her little Juliet balcony, or leaning out the apartment window, overlooking the street. When considered in the collective, we quickly scale up to a neighborhood association of Italian grandmothers, or "nonnas," who together form a formidable surveillance network — the envy of any police unit or intelligence agency. Indeed, the security camera is merely an objectified neighborhood watch program. For some, the security camera is a form of reassurance: a benign chaperone, or a "big brother" in the more friendly, familial sense. For others, it is a narc, poking its metallic nose into business that by rights should not be captured and logged for future reference.

Today, security cameras are not only installed by government officials or large faceless corporations, but also by friends, neighbors, and indeed ourselves. For less than the price of a decent lunch, we can install a security camera inside the home or next to our front door. Amazon's smart doorbell, Ring, for instance, allows us to watch the comings and goings outside our home even if we happen to be traveling overseas (thanks to the global magic of apps). For this reason, no babysitter or domestic help can perform her duties without presuming her employer is tracking her every move via a discreetly placed "nanny cam." And this places all of us into a defensive, pre-emptive mode of being in which we can't simply exist, but must anticipate being scrutinized and analyzed. Our attention is thus pulled outside our own minds and bodies so that we can watch ourselves in kind, as if navigating the world through a prosthetic periscope.

Indeed, the low-res visual regime of the security cam has led to a whole new aesthetic, processing the world through the cold and "objective" view of the surveillance camera.[3] The successful film franchise Paranormal Activity, for instance, rendered a new twist on the horror genre by showing most of the spooky events through a degraded digital filter, importing the old "magic lantern" world of shadowy ghosts into the fuzzy and impersonal plasma screen of pixels. The surveillance camera pays attention in a way that brings to mind the voyeur, but which is — initially at least — unconnected to the libido. Vulnerability is built into the system, however, which needs only a lone unscrupulous human to complete the circuit and exploit the infrastructure for his own secret, scopophilic pleasures (as depicted in the sleazy 1993 film Sliver). The security camera, in other words, is more or less begging to be hacked. Indeed, we are all possible targets of a remote voyeur thanks to the tiny surveillance cameras now installed in all our computers. As an inherently curious — and thus voyeuristic — species, our human senses tingle whenever we

---

3   See the artwork of Harun Farocki and Hito Steyerl.

DOMINIC PETTMAN

see security cam footage that may be capturing something salacious, scandalous, or simply ridiculous. (An unhealthy percentage of viral videos, for instance, are culled from warehouse or Ring footage of workers slacking off, falling over, making spectacular mistakes, or being menaced by pets.)

The surveillance camera's optic nerve often connects to a remote monitor, allowing humans to observe the footage. Such monitors, however, tend to multiply into banks, such that a security guard is obliged to pay attention to many screens at once. Thus, what in the 1970s signified a fractured kind of madness (personified by David Bowie in *The Man Who Fell to Earth*, watching as many TVs as he could, all at the same time), becomes — a few decades later — a banal, albeit impossible job description. The surveillance camera expands the attention ecology to an unprecedented degree, to the extent that we might even talk about a mirror world of cam footage, doubling what there is to be seen of life. Truly, the map of the globe is beginning to overlay the territory at a scale of 1:1. (And when we add the fact of our smartphones, we also can recognize a reserve army of electronic eyes, ready to deploy at any moment.)

Security cam footage — through its harsh, objective aesthetic — signifies "reality," even as its cynical ubiquity threatens to dissolve any lingering connection to the Real. We become addicted to this aesthetic because it gives us a glimpse of what it must be like to be an all-seeing God. It suggests raw, unfiltered, unedited access to life, allowing us to peer behind the curtains and see behind the performance: to find out *what's really going on.*[4] On a simple level, the CCTV system —

---

4   One pleasing use of security cams — especially in the age of extended lockdowns — is the website Window-Swap.com, which

and its digital progeny — gives us more and more "content" to pay attention to, and as a result, this precious and limited resource is spread even thinner. On a more conceptual level, however, the security cam represents a technological symptom of a deep *in*security and unease (to the extent that we might well change the name to "insecurity camera"). Menaced by the specter of terrorism, crime, trespassers, rule breakers, and shady behavior[5] — and indeed the proximity of "undesirable people" — the monitor of the CCTV camera recalls the hall monitor of our school days, but in a global, more vigilant — and infinitely more paranoid — way. The security cam is what happens when we outsource our most anxious suspicions to technology, and ask our machines to pay careful attention for us. This in turn encourages the medium itself to become paranoid, since it has been designed and instructed to find and record wrongdoing. Its attention, in other words, is highly overdetermined by the presumption of guilt (a reversal of our professed legal ethos). Under the gaze of the digital recording angel, we are at once anonymized — as a generic human

---

allows a computer user to peer through a remote window, often on the other side of the world, if they are bored of the view from their own.

5   It is believed that the term "shady" comes from the extralegal behavior that thrived underneath the elevated railway lines in nineteenth- and early twentieth-century New York — an elongated space in which people could interact in the shadows, with less fear of being observed. Indeed, it is a sign of our different values today that so many boast of being "seen," as if this is an inherently desirable thing, rather than preferring their assignations to be in the shadows.

unit — and singled out as a potentially delineated "person of interest."

The security cam — like the "confession cam" of reality TV — *produces* guilt or unsavory activity rather than simply recording it. It is like the famous observer in quantum physics, whose simple presence, as witness, influences the behavior of different sub-atomic particles. This now iconic object of soft-dystopian modern life is a potent symbol of the troubles that come with attempts at "full transparency," and of the dark irony that the more we attempt to safeguard our own welfare and liberty, the more we create the conditions for suffocating the same.

In sum, the security cam is an unblinking metallic cyclops, broadcasting the mundane activities of a species that squints suspiciously at each other before lurching into the future with eyes wide shut.

The Self-Driving Car

The self-driving car pays attention to its environment, via the digital sensorium of its programming. It scans the immediate environment in relation to its destination, and in doing so it identifies and analyzes all the manifold objects, options, and contingencies that lie between the one and the other. The self-driving car registers *everything* in the vicinity — a kind of democracy of objects[1] — even as it coordinates with GPS satellites, proprietary databases, and an invisible web of other intricate systems, all feeding it possibly relevant information in real time. (This is in sharp contrast to a human, whose inherited phenomenological "wetware" assumes that most of the world is essentially background scenery and thus safe to ignore, and who only notices the minimum of elements needed in order to maneuver from one place to the next.) The self-driving car is thus something of a metaphysical conundrum, since it — and the pronoun is surely appropriate here — does not in fact enjoy any kind of "self" or "selfhood" (at least, not any kind that the philosophers would recognize). Indeed, a more accurate name might be "driverless chauffeuring mechanism."[2]

---

1   See Levi Bryant's book of the same name (Open Humanities Press, 2011).

2   Sadly, the boffins building and promoting these things are increasingly opting for "autonomous vehicle."

In both his scientific and theological writings, Aristotle famously proposed a model of the cosmos that begins with a "prime mover," or "that which moves without being moved." In trying to puzzle out the nature of fundamental universal laws — laws regarding change, potentiality, motility, decay, and so on — Aristotle found that he needed the notion of a *first cause*: something that sets the universe, and all the elements that comprise it, in motion through its own volition. Ultimately, he decided that this initial catalyst — this originary animating principle — can only be a divine force, since all earthly examples appear to need the goading of an external force, or other modes of proto-thermodynamic assistance (even living animals need food as fuel and the resistance of terrestrial traction to move about). It would be intriguing, then, to discover where the celebrated sage would place the next-generation Tesla — or whichever company wins the current race to create these new machines[3] — within his classical understanding of physics if we had some way of introducing it to him.[4] For while Aristotle placed the prime mover in the inky void beyond the stars — since even they presumably need a bit of a push to move around the sky — the sudden, confronting sight of a self-driving vehicle would likely have sent the philosopher scampering back to his wax tablet to begin his cosmology afresh.

At any rate, the SDC (as we shall now call it for convenience) is an illuminating case study in the emerging world of what

---

3   "More than 80 companies are testing over 1,400 self-driving cars in the U.S.": https://www.natlawreview.com/article/driverless-car-accidents-who-s-fault

4   We may be tempted to think of the self-driving car as Wheels 3.0 after the carriage and the subsequent "horseless carriage."

we might call "artificial attention." It comes pre-populated with millions of maps, microsensors, algorithmic detection devices, and mind-boggling decision rhizomes designed to mimic the mostly unconscious actions and reactions of any given human driver. The information architects responsible for navigation and safety must anticipate, code, and preload practically every possible object, action, reaction, and situation that the vehicle may encounter, along with the requisite responses. Not only that, they must do so in order of possibility and/or desirability. Essentially, the software engineers follow the classical logical-conditional structure: "If X, then Y" (where X is anything from a faded stop sign, to a scampering dog, to an approaching tornado, and Y designates the proper automated actions, in order of preference, given all the other factors at play). At this point, we may legitimately question whether such programming — and the elaborate subroutines it provokes — really qualifies as a form of attention. Isn't this merely a neat mathematical trick, *simulating* attention?

Before we rush to answer such questions, we would do well to remember that similar condescending distinctions have long been applied to our animal friends, whom we have historically tended to consider similarly "machinic" in terms of their biologically hardwired instincts or simple evolutionary reactions (in contrast to the presumed superior nuance and freedom of human "responses"). The closer we look at such semantic presumption, however, the more dubious these distinctions become, especially when we admit that contemporary cognitive research is starting to reveal the full extent to which we ourselves tend to run on autopilot — relying on reptilian reservoirs and mammalian muscle memories to get through much of life.

Indeed, we could even be tempted into making the perverse argument that SDCs are obliged to explicitly, if not consciously, pay *more* attention to the environment than we do, since they are not equipped with the psychological and cultural templates we rely on to free up our own personal RAM for other things (more important things, such as obsessing over whether we talked to much at that party last Thursday, or whether today's underwear has already been asked to provide more noble service than it is structurally capable of). From this perspective, the SDC is like the protagonist of the famous Borges short story "Funes the Memorious," in which the titular character is tortured by a perfect memory — so perfect that it cannot be distinguished from pure perception. In the case of Funes, every external stimulus is logged and archived in plain sight; every single hair on anyone's head can be instantly recalled in painfully exquisite detail. Mercifully, very few of us suffer from photographic memories, and this allows us the precious mental space we need to daydream, misremember, speculate, and so on. Such faulty attempts to recollect our own pasts are in fact the building blocks of our own continuity and creativity — the latter retroactively forging a sense of the former. This is what we might call "the Proustian paradox." This is to say, the more we try to remember something fuzzy from our past — recall it into a kind of clarity — the more the past is "alive" to us as a phantom of itself. The past returns to us across a belated bridge of our own invention, rather than as sheer persistence (which, as Borges understood, would be indistinguishable from a haunting). Indeed, if we had perfect and total recall — as the SDC would be obliged to have — the past would not even be experienced as past, but more as a traumatic, stubborn, never-ending present.

Whether the SDC suffers from such information overload we can leave to the budding technological ethicists to argue (including any latter-day Jeremy Bentham seduced into asking the question: "Can the machine feel pain?").[5] We might also question the extent to which an SDC understands the precious nature of its cargo — a human passenger or passengers, in contrast to, say, a pile of packages from Amazon containing toxic plastic novelty toys. Presumably, the SDC is programmed to make as safe and punctual a journey as possible, no matter whether the passenger is the King of England or a Styrofoam clam-package stuffed with substandard pork dumplings delivered by Uber Eats (without presuming the value of one over the other — especially if you happen to have the munchies).

No matter how comprehensive the informational infrastructure, however, there are bound to be mistakes, as we have already seen, in early tests — especially those involving autopilot systems, like the ones installed in new-model Teslas (affording a kind of self-driving option with an instant-override switch). As I write, the National Highway Traffic Safety Administration is investigating this new technology, prompted by a run of accidents involving the "assisted-driving system" in which it steered itself into "parked fire trucks,

---

5 A whimsical art project by Joey Lee and Benedikt Groß attempts to place humans in the position of an SDC. In their own words, "'Who Wants to be a Self-driving Car?' is a data driven trust exercise that uses augmented reality to help people empathise with self-driving vehicle systems." https://benedikt-gross.de/projects/who-wants-to-be-a-self-driving-car

police cars and other emergency vehicles."[6] (Sadly, at least three people to date have sacrificed their lives in the cause of early adoption.)

Given these (only occasionally fatal) "teething problems" — and given the deafening absence of interest in driverless cars from the general public — how can we account for the mad rush to build them? How do we explain the industry push for this technology given that there are surely more pressing directions and projects to pour billions of dollars into, such as a cure for cancer or a global plan to mitigate climate catastrophe. Even the promotional spin around these "smart" vehicles seems to start on a defensive footing, since nobody has driverless cars on the top of their wish list other than the snake oil salesmen of Silicon Valley (and this alone, of course, should make us suspicious of their motives). The car, after all, is often considered *the* totem of American life (along with the gun),[7] and the specifically American "pursuit of happiness" is premised on the private, individual freedom to hit the road and to point the fender in whichever direction Johnny Citizen thinks his fate or fantasy lies (even if that direction only leads

---

6   https://www.nytimes.com/2021/08/16/business/tesla-autopilot-nhtsa.html

7   Consider how the semiotician Clotaire Rapaille was paid a fortune to crack the "code" of the American spirit animal when he convinced the makers of the Jeep to change their headlights from square to round in order to mimic the horse — that pioneering ancestor of the car (also embodied in the Ford Bronco, Mustang, and so on). In a more recent development of this theme, Jaguar Land Rover has placed "virtual eyes" on its SDCs to "make direct 'eye contact' with pedestrians to signal intent": https://www.businessinsider.com/jaguar-land-rover-eyes-on-cars-see-humans-trust-them-2019-9

to a fiery end, as we saw with James Dean, in real life, and in *Thelma & Louise*, on the silver screen).[8]

So, again: Why this strong push by the tech industry to wrench the honest and calloused hands of the red-blooded American driver from the steering wheel — that sensual symbol of Ayn Randian agency? The answer, of course, lies in the potential for profits through greater command, control, centralization, and captivation (the four Cs of twenty-first-century cybernetics). If our eyes are freed from the obligation to watch the road, they are more than likely going to caress the screens of digital portals, as the windshield is now freed up to repurpose itself as a giant interactive screen à la *Minority Report*. If we are no longer obliged to pay attention to other cars, street signs, traffic signals, and so forth, then we can increase our TOD even further (that is, our time-on-device — a highly measurable and profitable commodity). Indeed, we won't just be sitting passively in the back seat, doom-scrolling through our phones, but living inside a mobile computer. The car will no longer be just a car, but an "intelligent interface," zooming up and down alongside the other technological bubbles (zooming in both senses). We will travel to work and back — or to our friend's house and back — inside themed virtual environments, simulating forests, canonical paintings, Disney landscapes, or alien worlds featured in the Star Wars universe (paying extra, of course, to avoid incessant pop-up ads). Our eye movements will be tracked and recorded for enhanced engagement, and our every word — typed or spoken — will be logged and analyzed to further refine the frighteningly detailed profile the informatic priesthood

---

8   Certainly, Thelma and Louise would have finished on a less tragic note if they had chosen to go on the lam in an SDC.

already have of our tastes, moods, opinions, networks, and behavior. Indeed, why would Big Tech be satisfied with the limited attention-share of stationary roadside billboards when potential customers can suddenly find themselves *englobed inside* mobile equivalents — animated, all-immersive advertising — shuttling to and fro inside their own personal Times Square.

Given this rather transparent ploy for absolute access to every fiber of our being, it is remarkable how many people consider the smooth introduction and imminent ubiquity of SDCs to be inevitable. For if America, the land of the NASCAR gas-guzzling gearhead, is not actively resisting this corporate annexing of fast and furious masculinity, then the rest of the world will swiftly fall into line. This is indeed the wet dream of the Zuckerbergs, the Bezoses, and the Musks: a complete fusion of the actual highway with what may once again be dubbed "the information superhighway" now that cars and computers are essentially interchangeable. Never before has the dystopian scenario featured in the Pixar film *WALL-E* — in which obese humans whisk from one place to the next on zippy hover-beds, that double as computer screens — seemed so imminent.[9]

In short, the SDC involves an attentional mise en abyme, with different types and layers of attention nested inside the other like Russian dolls. We have the SDC itself, scanning the environment and navigating through it. We have a vast global infrastructure, including an army of satellites, following the

---

9   While acknowledging the irony that Pixar, now a Disney concern, is playing its significant part in bringing this dystopian scenario into being, as any parent who has resorted to streaming animated movies to placate their grizzling children can attest.

SDC on its journey, logging thousands of data points per second. We have the media interface of the vehicle-cum-computer, scanning the passenger for biometric information just as the passenger scans the internal screens for his or her own information-gathering purposes. Each SDC is thus a mobile microcosm of the world itself in the high digital era: a kind of cybernetic, posthuman centipede.

The Virus

The virus pays attention to any and all opportunities for self-replication. Famously, the virus is not "alive" in the sense that we think of animals, plants, or even bacteria as being alive. Rather, this "submicroscopic" agent dwells in some shadowy and mindless netherworld — between the quick and the dead — intent, nevertheless, on perpetuating itself at the expense of its hosts (in this sense, the virus can be indistinguishable from the typical Australian backpacker). The virus can be extremely patient, waiting for millennia in some cases for the right moment to infect an accommodating cell and reassemble itself from merely a dormant reservoir of basic genetic material into a fully functioning factory equipped with the instructions for its own reproduction and transmission. Some microbiologists believe that viruses originated as pieces of DNA that shuttled between cells but which, for whatever reason, went rogue in order to further their own mysterious agenda. Others in the same field argue that viruses most likely emerged as a mutation of early bacteria. In any case, whatever their origin or motive, their *mission* — mysterious as it is — has been most successful, since viruses outnumber every other biological entity whatsoever.[1]

---

1   Although, again, the taxonomic designation of the virus as "biological" — that is, as a living thing — is very much up for debate. EP Rybicki, for instance, has essentially described the virus as being life-adjacent, inhabiting the twilight regions at the outer

The question of attention may seem moot in the case of the virus since it lacks a brain, a perceptual framework, an organic sensorium, a nervous system, and even a fundamental cell structure (the latter considered by many scientists to be the bare minimum requirement for even the most passing entry into the great Book of Life). And yet the virus is forever on some kind of eyeless equivalent of "the lookout" for opportunities to spread itself through the general population. It seems to instinctively "know" how to efficiently transport itself from one body to another (or at least it fosters the conditions for its own transmission). In order to encourage such replication, the virus hitches a ride on what is known as a "vector," that is, a line of transmission between points in a diagram of infection. ("To the vector goes the spoils," is an old saying in the world of the virus, perhaps.) Some vectors may be insects, such as mosquitos, which carry the West Nile virus from one person to another. Some vectors are airborne, as with the flu, while others are created through the sharing of bodily fluids, like with HIV. So while it may be a stretch to say that the virus "pays attention" to the various vectors through which it travels, we would also be missing something if we were to deny this ambitious antagonist *some* kind of cryptic agency in the general attention ecology of biological existence.[2]

Indeed, it is this "vectorian" aspect that makes the virus so amenable to metaphoric appropriation. The computer

---

"edge of life." (See "The classification of organisms at the edge of life, or problems with virus systematics," *South African Journal of Science*. 1990, 86, pp. 182–86.)

2   Bruno Latour's work has been highly influential in terms of granting agency to non-human "actants."

virus, for instance, is not simply a figurative application of the original viroid model; it utilizes the same model of vector-based self-replication as its biological equivalent — albeit in the digital realm rather than the organic one. Here, the "informational" aspect of the biological virus is stripped down to its essence in the cybernetic context. And while techno-theorists — as well as the denizens of Silicon Valley — can be too quick to completely conflate these two types of infection, they can only get away with doing so because there is such a structural correspondence, or formal parallel, between the viruses found in the natural world and the ones found in the welcoming ecosystem of the Internet.[3]

The virus calls into question our assumptions about the relationship between attention and *in*tention, since we so often assume the former requires a healthy dose of the latter. The common cold, for instance, may not *want* to give you a sore throat, a runny nose, and a terrible cough — at least not in any psychological, anthropomorphic sense. However, it still "understands" the best, most effective, and efficient ways to do so (in the sense that such "understanding" is built into its self-replicating architecture rather than any cognitive apparatus,

---

3   The rather tragic Internet pioneer John McAfee — who died in 2021 in controversial circumstances in a jail cell in Barcelona — made his fortune from being one of the first people to create and license anti-virus software for personal computers. Recovering cyberpunk novelist Neal Stephenson speculated in his entertaining novel *Snow Crash* about a near-future when infected computers would learn to "crash" their human users as well (a feeling most of us can relate to, at least on some uncanny, symbiotic, and psychosomatic level where we ourselves feel ill when our computer has been commandeered or compromised by malware).

of which it has none). The transmission of the virus — and even the history of evolution itself — looks very different if we entertain the possibility that there is a form of attention that is not located in the individual, per se, as a faculty or skill, but in the holistic system or milieu itself (after all, nothing is more "transindividual" than a virus). This can even be seen in the etymology of the word "attention," which originates in the Latin *attendere*, to "give heed to," or literally, "to stretch toward." The virus — like its more urbane cousin, the parasite — *stretches toward* the environment or entity most conducive to sustaining and maintaining it.[4] What new perspectives or insights might be gleaned if we consider this a form of effective (albeit mindless) attention? Usually we associate our key term with a mindful focus, a kind of stationary reckoning with (or beckoning of) the world. From the radically new angle suggested by the virus, however, attention can be *an environmental product* of — a specific emergence from— the way different elements interact with each other (sometimes being in harmony, as with symbiosis, and other times agonistic, as with infection). Attention, in this instance, is not a cultivated capacity, but a blind drive, a rapacity.

This is partly what Richard Dawkins meant when he first proposed his famously provocative conceit of "the selfish gene." Rather than placing human individuals on the main stage of history, Dawkins suggests that we are little more than fleshy suitcases, designed to carry genetic material forward into the future (and for the sake of the material itself, rather than our own). From this perspective, we are suddenly demoted from the apex of life — the apotheosis of evolutionary experimentation —

---

4   Michel Serres, *The Parasite* (Minneapolis: University of Minnesota Press, 2007).

and made humble couriers for the genome itself. In such a theory, Dawkins almost betrays a sadistic undertone of glee as he regretfully informs us that our feelings and accomplishments mean precisely nothing compared to the DNA instructions that we pass on to the next generation (instructions that most of us are far too ignorant to even read, let alone comprehend). Again, from this disorienting viewpoint, our great passions are but opportunistic ruses, alibis, excuses, and Trojan horses to keep the selfish gene in circulation; our most meaningful love affairs just a Darwinian trick to convince our shy procreative equipment to bloody well do its job.

It is notable, then, just as we saw with the self-driving car, that something with no sense of selfhood — in this case the miniscule double helix — can still be considered somehow self-centered, if not downright selfish. After dropping this initial bombshell, Dawkins, later in the same book, further erodes the presumptions of human agency by proposing a *cultural* equivalent to genetic proliferation, which he calls the "meme."[5] This he defined as a "cultural unit of transmission" which spreads from person to person in a manner suspiciously akin to a virus. Again, from this anti-humanist perspective, everything from fashion, to art, to gestures, to wolf whistles, to complex modes of thinking is little more than a "memetic" phenomenon — trans-generational symptoms of cultural contagion. Such a view even recalls science fiction scenarios, such as the one suggested by William Burroughs in which language itself is a virus.[6]

---

5   For this new term, Dawkins adapted the ancient Greek word *mīmēma*, meaning "imitated thing."

6   For Burroughs, the linguistic virus originates in outer space. But we need not evoke a panspermia theory of language in order to

Today, the popular definition of a "meme" has narrowed and crystallized into those didactic images we encounter and share on social media, deliberately designed for maximum transmissibility (with most memes using the vector of either humor or anger in order to foster the necessary affective motivation for the host to pass the image along the network). Politically speaking, memes are a kind of media virus, often infecting those exposed to them with either a new or a weaponized ideology, such as Trumpism, on the one side, or so-called *wokeism*, on the other.[7] The digital ecosystem of the Internet appears to be custom built for the smooth and rapid circulation of these media viruses and their various mutations and novel strains. (Memetic viruses seem to proliferate especially well within the labyrinthine tunnels of online rabbit holes.) Moreover, some users — Boomers on Facebook, for instance, or young incels on Reddit — are depicted, fairly or not, as typical superspreaders of misinformation, paying attention to bad vectors and opening up new ones. (The search for patient zero of whichever case is making headlines in any given week usually locates the culprit either in Russia or at some dubious IP address connected to a well-funded Super PAC based in the American Bible Belt.)

In any case, the exceedingly promiscuous adaptability of the viral motif only further underscores the extent to which virality itself, or transmissibility *per se*, is an ur-model for comprehending such essential processes as change or influence (or rather, change *as* influence). "Virus" names not

---

acknowledge the highly memetic aspect of our spoken and written forms of communication.

7   Douglas   Rushkoff,   *Media   Virus!*   (New   York: Ballantine Books, 1994).

just the wily RNA sequence, or the malicious computer code, but any operation or exchange that threatens the integrity — real or imagined — of a host organism. Like a dye injected into a mobile system in order to better map and visualize its components and connections, the viral vector is a diagram — both abstract and actual — tracing connections between elements that seemingly had no previous relationship (elements such as a senator from Alabama and a bat from a wet market in Wuhan; or in the case of something "going viral" online, between a Nigerian teenager dancing in her room on TikTok and the marketing company that seeks to monetize the same dance, without compensation, in a new worldwide campaign).[8]

As I write, the coronavirus has been causing havoc throughout the world for over eighteen months. The worst pandemic in a century has killed millions, sickened hundreds of millions, and sent economies — and even basic social interactions — into a strange state of suspended animation. And while vaccines were developed and distributed (in some countries, at least) in record time, Covid has proven too ubiquitous, and too sly — morphing into turbo-charged versions of itself, such as the dreaded Delta variant — to be vanquished by the likes of Pfizer. (Perhaps this is just a foretaste of worse to come.) Many commentators have

---

8   Ultimately, the virus can seemingly work against its own interest, since the more fatal the strain, the lower its chances of infecting new bodies. In this sense, we might compare the virus with the counter-intuitive designs of the 1 percent — that parasitical economic class who often seem more intent on killing the host that sustains them than ensuring even a minimum of health in the social body in order to enable further feeding into the future.

marveled at how a tiny scrap of protein — so small that it cannot even be detected by microscopes — can bring empires, and even the mighty human race itself, to their knees (surely a long-overdue biological lesson in hubris, perhaps designed by Gaia herself). The new vaccines were explained to us as a crash course designed to teach the human body's natural defense mechanisms to recognize and neutralize this hitherto unknown intruder. They thus have a pedagogical intent, which in turn suggests that the vaccines encourage the body to *pay attention* — to bone up about this new foe that threatens its life and well-being. In this scenario — complicating, again, the notion of attention as a form of willpower or psychological focus — the new antibodies are the genetic result of an accelerated *biological* type of attention, one which circulates in an attention ecology beyond the frame of personal application or aptitude. And as such, the war — the arms race — between virus and immune system is ultimately won by whichever antagonist pays the most effective attention to the wiles and machinations of the other.

Whether the coronavirus will eventually be shown to have originated in a laboratory leak or a crowded market full of exotic animals matters little now that the tiny genie is out of the bottle. What the pandemic represents, however, is the pressing urgency of paying attention to our own location, role, and behavior in relation to both the world's organic ecosystems and the technological infrastructure which now covers the world with its sticky fiber-optic webs. Only by relinquishing our own selfish ways — including the geographic hoarding of antiviral technologies — will we have even half a chance of meeting this selfish biological meme halfway.

The Astronomer

The astronomer pays attention to signals from the deepest reaches of the cosmos. He does so with the aid of enormous prostheses that magnify his eyes and amplify his ears a billionfold. Like a tiny, patient, nocturnal insect, he sits among telescopes and satellite dishes looking and listening for various signs: indications of anomalous activity, for instance, or the verifications of new theories concerning the complex movement of heavenly bodies. These he scribbles down for future consultation.

The astronomer is yet another ambiguous figure. On the one hand, he brings us a profound sense of wonder as a virtual traveler exploring the reaches of time and space. He is a diplomat — a modern day Marco Polo — bringing back strange news of strange new lands and fantastic descriptions of exotic artifacts from the frontiers of alien worlds. On the other hand, he brings us an equally profound sense of melancholia, consistently confirming our suspicion that there seems to be no other life beyond our tiny smudge of biospheric marmalade, spread thin and fragile over the Earth's crust. In short, he can charm our restless spirits with epic tales of extraterrestrial discovery, and — in the next breath — deliver a harsh reality check concerning the meaningless fluke of our preposterous existence. It is this uneasy, seemingly contradictory coexistence of humility and hubris that the astronomer provokes with his squint-eyed observations.

Dwelling on the more heartening aspect for a moment, the astronomer is a symbol of humanity's almost divine capacity to witness the infinite mystery of the universe, to explain some of its workings, and to name some of its more mysterious phenomena. He can soothe our sense of isolation — our nagging cosmic loneliness — by reassuring us that there are billions and billions of stars out there, scattered through the unthinkable reaches of space, each one with the potential to support an Earthlike planet and thus perhaps even an Earthlike ensemble of living beings.[1]

The symbolic gravity of the astronomer can be found in a once widely shared fable concerning an unnamed Enlightenment astronomer announcing the inauguration of a new Promethean telescope to an assembled crowd. Almost immediately, however, the stargazer is confronted by one of the attendees. "Isn't it true that such a presumptuous device serves to diminish our own role and sense of purpose in the universe, making us feel small and insignificant? Can't you admit that this rather blasphemous compulsion, peering into the corners of Eternity, reduces the works and existence of Man?" The humanistic response comes with a knowing smile and the significant lifting of an index finger: "Ah, but Man is the *astronomer!*" The moral of the fable is that *we* are the ones who have the incredible capacity to realize — and thus (potentially, at least) to make peace with — our own celestial parochialism (in contrast to every other creature on

---

1   As the world's beloved corduroy-clad scientific uncle, Carl Sagan, was fond of saying, we should marvel at the fact that we are literally made up of "starstuff" (that is to say, our atoms have already looped around the universe for billions of years, originating in the Big Bang itself).

Earth, simply going about their instinctual business — their snouts and antennae turned toward the ground, oblivious of the various fates and finitudes written in the stars). In this symbolic and highly didactic scenario, it is precisely our technically augmented attention, focused on the infinite expanse beyond our local ken, that allows us to transcend our own humble origins and thus level up into a kind of species-wide self-actualization. Finally, we see ourselves in a proper, universal context, even if that context is dark, silent, infinite, inscrutable, and — well — ultimately rather terrifying.

Since that distant day when our evolutionary ancestors decided to straighten our simian spines (in an attempt to create as great a distance as possible between our faces and our own feces, according to Freud), the human race has lifted its chin upward (a scene reenacted so memorably and allegorically by Arthur C. Clarke and Stanley Kubrick in *2001: A Space Odyssey*: the ape, bestowed with the name of Moonwatcher, turning his reflective gaze to the stars above). In ancient cultures and classical traditions, the astronomer was a central figure by virtue of this increasingly refined capacity to read the sky like so many glittering tea leaves (in contrast to today, when his main remaining prophetic duty is to warn world leaders if a meteorite may be on a collision course with Earth).[2]

In ancient Egypt, for instance, the astronomer was a geomancer, tracing enduring lines in the sand according to vectors whispered by the night sky into the ears of the Pharoah.

---

2   The current candidate for the asteroid with the highest chance of plummeting into our planet is Bennu: the likeliest impact coming on the afternoon of September 24, 2182 (with a 1 in 2700 chance of hitting Earth).

In ancient China, the astronomer tapped deep roots branching into Babylonian and Indian proto-scientific traditions. Later, in the Middle Ages, the Chinese learned much from Arabic astronomy, and vice versa.[3] In Aztec and Mayan cultures, he was the prime architect of entire cities, and of their intimate relation with the heavens, with which they were in constant conversation, with a special emphasis on auspicious sacrificial dates. In Neolithic Europe, he was the principal consultant in the arrangement of vast stone monuments, such as Stonehenge, while in medieval times, he could find himself a prisoner — or even suddenly bereft of the diminutive planetarium of his head — if he interpreted the movements of the constellations in a way which did not please his sponsor.[4] The Copernican shift in this exulted form of attention occurred, quite naturally, with Nicolaus Copernicus himself: an astronomer who — along with Galileo, half a century later — helped deliver an ego bruise from which humanity itself is still trying to recover. It was his 1543 bombshell *On the Revolutions of the Heavenly Spheres* which detailed the theory (and soon to be heresy) of heliocentrism, boldly stating that we are not in fact situated at the center of the universe but biding time in the cosmic

---

3   In ancient China, the job of astronomer was hereditary, and the office (in the Imperial Astronomical Bureau) involved not only celestial observation, but the trafficking of state secrets. A bad calculation could result in punishment up to and including death. Interestingly, each new dynasty would install or adapt an entirely new calendar based on the stars ("He who could give a calendar to the people would become their leader").

4   Today, the astronomer has lost his quasi-sacred status, even as his knowledge is valued much more highly than that of the astrologer (in polite company, at least).

equivalent of a semi-abandoned strip mall in suburban New Zealand.[5]

Today, the astronomer enjoys less power and consequence than in former times, though he is still occasionally trotted out for podcasts or panel shows to lend some gravitas to the occasion. Nevertheless, he diligently continues his work without the fanfare or glamor of centuries past, using instruments exponentially more powerful than the ones used by those celebrated historical personages we've just been discussing. (What's more, he does so with mathematical accuracy and in detail that would blow their scientific minds.) More than any other figure in this exhibition of attentional types, the astronomer's attention is located beyond the here and now — stretched as far as modern science will allow — as he peers deep into both time and space (since these are, as Einstein understood, two words designating different perspectives on the same thing). The astronomer is unique in the unfathomable remoteness, speed, size, and alien aspect of his objects of fascination, as well as in the trajectories they describe. He is thus matched only by the particle physicist, who fixates her attention in the opposite direction, diving down deep into the elementary texture of things thanks to the unblinking and piercing eye of electron microscopes, peering into the hidden folds of our own world, revealing spacious microcosms inhabited by lonely sub-atomic particles. For while the meteorologist can lose her head in the clouds — and forget to pay attention to her own shoelaces or toaster — the astronomer and the particle physicist are apt to suffer the same kind of absent-mindedness, but on a much more epic scale,

---

5   Bruce Mazlish, *The Fourth Discontinuity: The Co-Evolution of Humans and Machines* (New Haven: Yale University Press, 1995).

given the fact that their attention muscles are trained in the taking of mind-bogglingly inhuman measurements, leaving such mundane matters as the human body in the distracted dust ("mundane" meaning "of the earth").

Modern theories of the universe — steeped in the deep weirdness of quantum physics, string theory, infinite-universe speculations, and so on — give little traction for our ongoing desire to feel existentially validated by the cosmos. For if God is dead and even Einstein's theories are looking quaint — or at least insufficient — then who, or what, are we to turn to in order to provide our immaterial existence with any kind of even fleeting meaning. As we proceed to trash the only planet we have — and as grotesque billionaires indulge in flaccid phalli-measuring competitions amid the Great Orbital Space-Debris Patch of dead and dying satellites — the astronomer has lost the magic authority he once enjoyed (an authority earned by virtue of his capacity to interpret the enigmatic text inked above our heads in starlight). As I write, Elon Musk has patented a new technology allowing advertising billboards to share "aerial real estate" with the moon. What kind of astronomical legacy can compete with such unfettered terrestrial vulgarity and greed? The only hope lies in the possibility that our attention is not so easily captured while our incurious noses are buried deep in our smartphones.

Perhaps the whole evolutionary pattern will have to reboot itself all over again: humanity 2.0. And just as Moonwatcher, the contemplative ape, lifted his head from his nightly foraging to gaze upon the inscrutable face of the luminous moon, some restless and sensitive soul of the near future will lift her head from her social media feed and suddenly be inspired to the point of epiphany by the SpaceX satellite high above, streaking across the light-polluted sky.

The Fool

The fool pays attention to things that most people fail to notice. As he is "soft in the head" — or at least pretends to be — the fool is free to focus on objects and situations that others find irrelevant or inappropriate. He can pay attention to spiders, dog poop, trashy TV shows, or online conspiracy theories, creating his own idiosyncratic (often also idiotic) attention ecology. The fool's head twitches this way and that, easily distracted by movement, color, sudden sounds, or the movement of the spheres themselves. (As the Beatles sing: "The fool on the hill sees the Sun going down / And the eyes in his head see the world spinning round.") As a consequence, the fool notices, and often draws attention to, things that other people likely notice but *fail to acknowledge* out of tact, discretion, or diplomacy, or in the interest of self-preservation.

The fool is an extremely capacious figure, capable of wearing many different, multicolored hats. The term itself – historically and inescapably ableist – can encompass everyone from the cognitively impaired, to the neurodivergent, to the merely eccentric, to the mainstream comedian inhabiting the role for the sake of a laugh. Historically speaking, the fool breathed a different type of oxygen to the village idiot, since the former entertained the sovereign in the royal court by dint of his sharp wit and wicked tongue. Hence the paradoxical character of the "wise fool," who populates medieval and early modern accounts of public life, and who functions as a kind of hinge between the feudal ways of the old world and the nascent tendency to "speak truth to power" that would eventually arrive in the formal guise of democracy and revolution.[1]

Today, the fool usually comes in two contrasting types: the buffoon (personified by Homer Simpson) and the aforementioned comedian (embodied by any stand-up performer you care to mention). The former is *actually* foolish — a modern version of the village idiot — while the latter derives from the court jester or clown and is knowingly "fooling around." Homer and his many brethren are dim-witted, credulous, and easily duped, while professional comedians are merely *playing* the fool for the flattering currency of the laugh. Both, however, are deeply imbricated in the attention economy of the foolhardy.

Perhaps the most representative stand-up comedian in this sense is Jerry Seinfeld, who has made a king's fortune with his own specific brand of observational humor: a kind of whimsical weaponizing of the act of paying attention. This comedic style has been reduced to its essence in the sarcastic, goggle-eyed, nasal refrain: "What's the deal with airline food?!" (As one character disparagingly asks Seinfeld in an episode of his TV show, "So you do that 'did you ever notice' kind of stuff?") The meta-humor here is created by the somewhat sheepish acknowledgment that much of the material, designed to be amusing, relies a great deal on sheer "relatability" rather than on the usual comedic techniques such as parody, satire, word play, implication, surrealism, surprise, transgression, and so on. ("Ha ha!" roars the audience. "What *is* the deal with

---

1   Some nineteenth-century Russian novels, including Tolstoy's *War & Peace*, note the presence of a "fool" in the midst of affluent, bourgeois families, who apparently saw the need of one in domestic service, along with a cook, a maid, and a coachman.

airline food?!") The joke hardly needs to be completed, as the punchline doubles as the setup.

The social role or symbolic function of the fool, however, loses its footing — reverses its magnetic polarity, we might say — if the king's throne is suddenly occupied by a clown, as has been happening with alarming frequency in the past decade or so. Beginning with Silvio Berlusconi in Italy, and reaching full insane-clown-posse proportions with Donald Trump and Boris Johnson, the village idiot has shown himself to be playing the long game. This is to say, after swallowing slights and insults for centuries, the jester has now seized power by virtue of his disarming disposition as overtly cartoonish. What's more, he now has the keys to the communicational infrastructure, defining the agenda, tone, and attention ecology of the masses.

How to proceed without panic in a world where jokers run wild in the corridors of power even as the building is on fire? One coping strategy is to put on the clown makeup oneself, as a kind of jeering defense mechanism. Indeed, a few minutes on social media suffice to confirm the extent to which dark humor is the global psychological crutch of the age. Even distinguished professors, or so I'm told, indulge in the increasingly popular online hobby of "shitposting." Such a response, however, merely fuels the flames of foolishness, for even highly educated commentaries on the topic du jour (decided in advance by the Twitter algorithm) tend to be reduced to the inherent stupidity of whatever accursed object has been deemed to be "trending" on any given day and offered up to the voracious and sacrificial economy of social media. After all, what is the point of being really smart about really stupid things?

In other words, it matters little how intelligent any given individual may be (and we all flatter ourselves, despite the math, that we are above average in this sense). "The discourse" is set up in such a way as to be implicitly and irredeemably the provenance of the fool. When it comes to clowns like Donald or Boris — and the rabid clown army who continue to carry the torch of their grotesque, burlesque performance — we cannot help but find ourselves swept along with the moronic current.[2] This is the lesson of both the medieval allegory of "the ship of fools" and of the now-classic film *Idiocracy* (which, as many have noted, was originally made as a satire, but which has since moved into the realm of prophetic documentary).

Stupidity has indeed been built into the very bones of the social body, and it is valuable to remind ourselves that, no matter how impressive our credentials, we all act like fools at some point or another, and with far more frequency than we realize (or at least care to admit).[3] The figure of the fool thus performs an essential social function, akin to the scapegoat. In this case, however, we do not *kill* someone marked as different for the greater social cohesion of the surviving members; rather, we laugh at them, or even *with* them, in an act of necessary catharsis and release. (As the old saying goes: "Fool me once, shame on you. Fool me twice, shame on me. Fool me thrice and you may sell out Madison Square Garden.")

---

2   We need not look to such *obvious* figures for contemporary avatars of the fool motif. After all, Jeff Bezos, Elon Musk, Richard Branson, and co. have proven themselves to be — despite and amid their obscene wealth — fools of the highest order, funding space elevators and fantastical colonies on Mars even as a fraction of the cost of these projects could save the world's infrastructure from sinking swiftly into the silt.

3   Bernard Stiegler, *States of Shock: Stupidity and Knowledge in the 21st Century* (Cambridge, UK: Polity, 2015).

The fool, like any good harlequin, has masks and Janus faces. He can, on the one hand, oblige us to pay attention to painful but important things by virtue of his keen sense of humor, which dulls the blade of difficult truth.[4] More often, on the other hand, he distracts us from what is important and muddies any clarity we may briefly enjoy in terms of responding to the crises at hand. The fool dominates the Tarot deck in an age when we are, to quote the media critic Neil Postman, "amusing ourselves to death." And as a consequence, we may be obliged to risk accusation of humorlessness if we're to escape the relentless, ubiquitous foolishness of the infinite-ringed media circus.

After all, we are only fooling ourselves if we try to deny the fact that we are *all* crammed into the one, single clown car, hurtling along the highway at a hundred miles an hour, sputtering oil and backfiring banana peels, and heading rapidly toward a cliff.

---

4   Desiderius Erasmus, *The Praise of Folly* (Princeton, NJ: Princeton University Press, 2015). First published in 1511. See also Lucian's highly influential satirical dialogues from the second century AD.

Attention Today

As you may have gleaned by now, this is not a book *about* paying attention. It is, instead, a collection of portraits, sketched with a free hand. Each portrait represents an attempt to figure, embody, and describe different ways of conjuring the mysterious act we call "paying attention." Whether it be the surfer, poet, influencer, massage therapist, or someone else altogether, there are as many ways of paying heed to the world as there are people with the capacity to do so (each of whom either refuses or takes up this challenge from moment to moment). We tend, in other words, to be engaged with specific slices of life in particularly idiosyncratic — even eccentric — ways. Indeed, many of us recognize our friends, loved ones, and enemies by the manner and style of their attending to things — whether this be manifest in their conversation, their clothing, their body language, or the unwritten signature inscribed in their works. Beyond the phenomenological invitation, however, offered to every individual by the environment or milieu we happen to find ourselves in, there are also *im*personal, generic, collective, inherited, and formalized ways of responding to what simply (or not so simply) *is*.

In the previous pages — in this gathering of types — I tried to inhabit, channel, and depict a selection of these more established modes of paying attention. And I did so in an effort to encourage a more mindful approach to our mindful capacities in general. (As Catherine Malabou asks, in a disarmingly straightforward provocation: "What should we do with our brain?")[1] We have, after all — and for a long time — been actively discouraged from paying attention to the act of paying attention. Instead, we've been solicited, seduced, hailed, hypnotized, entertained, influenced, coerced, distracted, blackmailed, notified, polled, prodded, and poked — increasingly by ubiquitous forms of digital media. It is no secret, of course, that our so-called attention spans have been shattered this side of the millennium. (The very idea of quantifying something as abstract as our power of attentiveness and measuring its "span" is itself a product of the modern age, which has simultaneously — and in parallel — done so much to frack and extract attention as a resource.)

I therefore consider this project part of a loose phalanx of relatively recent books that can be considered part of an emerging subfield of "attention studies." Inaugurated by Jonathan Crary in the early 1990s, more recent titles include Yves Citton's *The Ecology of Attention*, Paul North's *The Problem of Distraction*, Tim Wu's *The Attention Merchants*, and many others besides. My own contribution, on this occasion, does not seek a traditional scholarly understanding of its key term, but rather a more "pataphysical" appreciation of its presence in the cultural imaginary, its challenge to our own habitual modes of analysis, and the opportunities involved in "thinking otherwise" (outside the protocols of academic writing).

The book you are currently reading thus shares more in common with "untimely" books like Roland Barthes' *Mythologies* or Vilém Flusser's *Gestures*, which both experiment with highly targeted modes of poetic analysis. These texts

---

1   Catherine Malabou, *What Should We Do with Our Brain?* (Fordham University Press, 2008).

are not designed to have the last word in comprehensive comprehension. Instead, they demonstrate — or better, provide a proof of concept for — a different way of approaching any given micro-slice of cultural material. Whether it be margarine, striptease, smoking a pipe, or turning a mask around, Barthes and Flusser both understood that it can be just as rewarding, intellectually speaking, to draw rapid portraits of the lineaments of their chosen object as to nail them down to the conventions of historiography, hermeneutics, or ethnography. These meta-theorists understood that a different genre of writing would yield different insights and opportunities for illumination. A lighter touch can indeed generate new questions and novel directions, some of which may even bear conceptual fruit as nourishing as that arrived at through careful archival research or systematic theoretical reflection. In borrowing some of the tricks and tropes from the belles-lettres tradition, Barthes and Flusser (as well as more recent writers like Anne Carson and Maggie Nelson) created a hybrid genre: one that speaks with Janus tongues in two directions, attempting to intrigue the fabled "general reader" as much as instruct the scholar (and vice versa).[2] Such promiscuity can in turn generate new perspectives, new questions, new, more conversational relationships with the phenomena themselves.

Scholars are expected to pay attention to their chosen topics, sources, and fields in a certain way. There are very good reasons for this, especially in an age in which authority, reason, and even the verification of historical truths have given way to "alternative facts." The rapidly changing mediascape,

---

2   Carla Nappi has called this relatively novel methodology "fictioning." See Carla Nappi, "Metamorphoses: Fictioning and the Historian's Craft." *PMLA,* 133(1), 2018, pp. 160–165.

however, has — as Marshall McLuhan famously claimed — altered our sense ratios, our sensoria, and our capacities for navigating the world to the extent that people today may as well be a different *species* to the linear, rational "typographic Man" of yesteryear. Indeed, these two forms of navigating the world — let's call them the ink-stained hedgehog and the electric fox — are increasingly difficult to disentangle in our hyper-wired world. Academic attention is itself in the midst of a rapid transformation and upheaval. What does it mean, for instance, that ChatGPT can simulate academic authority in an increasingly convincing way? Moreover, what does this say about our cherished capacities for linguistic description and the congealed modes which we privilege as vectors of truth?

In summoning thirty different types to share the secrets of their orientation in relation to the world — or at least in imagining what these secrets might be, given my limited experience with each example — I'm also attempting (in solidarity with many others) to expand the possibilities of intellectual legitimacy and what we might call "creative criticality."

In his writings on action, the enlightened thinker Jiddu Krishnamurti made a rather crucial distinction between attention, on the one hand, and concentration, on the other. "Attention is not concentration," he insists.

> When you concentrate, as most people try to do — what takes place when you are concentrating? You are cutting yourself off, resisting, pushing away every thought except that one particular thought, that one particular action. So your concentration breeds resistance, and therefore concentration does not bring freedom.... But whereas if you are attentive, attentive to everything that

is going on about you, attentive to the dirt, the filth of the street, attentive to the bus which is so dirty; attentive [to] your words, your gestures, the way you talk to your boss, the way you talk to your servant, to the superior, to the inferior; the respect, the callousness to those below you, the words, the ideas — if you are attentive to all that, not correcting, then out of that attention you can know a different kind of concentration.[3]

For all its important and admirable qualities, then, traditional scholarship often conflates paying attention with prolonged concentration (as any haunted PhD student will tell you for the price of a stiff drink). The previous pages are thus an attempt to honor Krishnamurti's insight and distinction here, in the hope that "a different kind of concentration" might emerge. One that invites, rather than pushes away. One that opens up, rather than closes down.

***

For the past few years here in New York City, I have taught an interdisciplinary course for first-year college students called "Anti-Social Media: Attention, Distraction, Addiction." What I've learned from this experience is that it doesn't take much prompting to convince the younger generation that smartphones are a double-edged sword, at best, slicing through their attentional capacities with every notification. My students are very good at damning self-diagnosis. The hard

---

3   Jiddu Krishnamurti, *Action: A Selection of Passages from the Teachings of J. Krishnamurti* (The Krishnamurti Foundation of America, 1990), p. 70.

part comes in trying to think of ways to encourage various practices of sustained attention when so much of modern life is deliberately designed to work against monotasking, mindfulness, and other modes of being self-present (or indeed being present to the present itself).

Nevertheless, I did strike upon one exercise that I will call an unmitigated success, one I stole from the avant-garde writer Georges Perec (the same fellow who honed his own attention muscles by, in one famous instance, composing a lengthy novel without using the letter "e"). In the autumn of 1974, Perec penned a much shorter book, called *An Attempt at Exhausting a Place in Paris*, in which he makes a careful inventory of everything he notices while sitting in Saint-Sulpice Square. Admittedly, since he ventures no interpretation or even poetic description — but rather the bare bones of his attention — it makes for pretty dry reading.

> An 86 [bus] passes by. An 87 passes by. A 63 passes by
> People stumble. Micro-accidents.
> A 96 passes by. A 70 passes by.
> It is twenty after one.
> Return (uncertain) of previously seen individuals:
> a young boy in a navy blue peacoat holding a plastic
> bag in his hand passes by the café again
> An 86 passes by. An 86 passes by. A 63 passes by.
> The café is full
> On the plaza a child is taking his dog for a run (looks
> like Snowy)
> Right by the café, at the foot of the window and at three
> different spots, a fairly young man draws a sort of "V"
> on the sidewalk with chalk, with a kind of question
> mark inside it (land art?)

A 63 passes by
Six sewer workers (hard hats and high boots) take rue
des Canettes.
Two free taxis at the taxi stand
An 87 passes by[4]

(And so on… You get the idea.)

As a result, the students arrive in class after reading this homework in a less than excited frame of mind. "That was so boring!" comes the inevitable refrain, and they seem rather surprised when I agree with them. "Yes, tedious, isn't it," I concur. "Now go and do it for yourself. Go and try to exhaust a place in Greenwich Village." Usually, my charges respond to this instruction with a collective expression of distaste and surprise — as if I had just asked them to go and get me a cup of coffee. But first-year students, especially, being a *relatively* obedient species — that is, before a couple of years of critical thinking has truly activated their more bolshie neurons — pack up their notepads and pens (since we have banished electronic devices from this classroom, which is dedicated to the focusing of the mind) and slink out into the mean New York streets.

When the students return to the seminar room, ninety minutes later, it is truly remarkable how many of them are, after the initial resistance and eye-rolling, genuinely and touchingly grateful that they were not only given this task but given the *permission* to lift their eyes from their devices and take a gentle account of the world around them. Year after year, the majority of students cite this deceptively simple exercise as one of the highlights of the course and speak of a sudden

---

4   Georges Perec, *An Attempt at Exhausting a Place in Paris* (Cambridge, MA: Wakefield Press, 2010). p.12.

unexpected calm — a quieting of the mind and a swift hushing of the constant mental muzak of anxiety — once they turn off their phones and start to truly pay attention to the immediate environment around them. Suddenly NYC is not just a busy, blurry, whirling vortex — the almost CGI-like background of their "main character syndrome" — but a highly specific space and time, populated by all sorts of interesting characters, as well as by suggestive signs of stories in progress — if we only take the time to notice them. And it comes as a genuine revelation to my students that this unfamiliar feeling — a mix of presence, curiosity, receptivity, and creativity — can be accessed so readily, at any time or place, without too much effort (although many confess to eventually being seduced back to their text messages or social media feeds).

What I myself have learned from setting this exercise is not exactly surprising: what a twentieth-century person might take for granted — the observational and speculative pleasures of people-watching, or of just watching the world go by — is a rapidly dying art in the age of constant connection, nudge notifications, and aggressive "engagement." Indeed, unless we *consciously* and *conscientiously* push back — or better, *step* back — we are likely to be "amused to death" in ways and through new media that the critic who coined this phrase in the first place could not have even imagined (Neil Postman having penned his bleak assessment of our continuing susceptibility to the logic of bread and circuses — with a strong preference for the latter — more than a decade before the Internet and so-called social media came into popular use).[5] At any rate, while for my students the leap

---

5   Neil Postman, *Amusing Ourselves to Death: Public Discourse in the Age of Show Business* (New York: Penguin, 1985). The primary

toward full *sonder* may still be some time away,[6] they have hopefully established the mental muscle memory necessary to allow them to eventually step beyond the isolating (albeit networked), self-generated bubble of "the digital enclosure."[7] Indeed, the stakes are high, since only if they — if we — can successfully initiate such a seemingly small step will we in fact encourage a "great leap" for mediated kind: a leap that can help the next generation go beyond "exhausting" their environment and start creating new spaces and ways to exhaust the world in satisfying, liberating, and nourishing ways. (For there are few things more satisfying in life than the kind of exhaustion that follows honest efforts, shared activities, inclusive conspiracies, and collective squanderings.)

***

Truth be told, however, I often feel guilty — as an educator — for encouraging my students to pay closer attention to things. After all, the more you pay attention to the world — whether it's the news, the environment, or the passive-aggressive

---

villain in Postman's argument is television. Indeed, we should not today presume to have escaped the clutches of "the idiot box" just because we can now carry it around in our pockets.

6   "Sonder" is an increasingly popular neologism coined by *The Dictionary of Obscure Sorrows* and defined as "the realization that each random passerby is living a life as vivid and complex as your own." https://www.dictionaryofobscuresorrows.com/post/23536922667/sonder

7   Mark Andrejevic, *Reality TV: The Work of Being Watched* (New York: Rowman & Littlefield, 2004).

theme park of family communication — the more difficult it is not to become disheartened, stressed out, or downright depressed. Attention leads to knowledge, and knowledge can be a heavy burden. Consciousness can feel like a curse, especially in an age as lost and unforgiving as this one, which in turn explains why we sometimes envy the animals their blessed ignorance of tomorrow and the apprehension that planning for it can bring (the squirrel's scramble for nuts notwithstanding).

But consciousness can also be a gift, since it allows us — at least in our better moments — to *truly live* rather than to simply exist. But how are we to judge the difference between these two ontological modes? One answer — the rather smug humanist one — would be to emphasize our engagement with *art* over and above the mere existential tarrying of other creatures. In this view, art is elevated as a semi-divine gift that allows us to savor the sweet nectar of expression, as well as the nourishing ambrosia of profound communication, before we shuffle off this mortal coil. In this scenario, every kind of creative activity helps us rise above the rushing river of meaningless temporality, as we redeem our fleeting consciousness in various considered acts of self-reflection (hence the primary philosophical imperative to live the examined life: "Know thyself"). The *better* answer, at least in my view, is not to valorize the arts by holding them aloft and apart, but by cultivating and celebrating the multisensory forms of auto-poesis that we share with *all* living things. Paradoxically, perhaps, our fellow creatures can be our teachers here, since — undistracted by overthinking and second-guessing — they presumably relish sensual immersion in the world in more profound and uncompromised ways than we can (at least in between those frantic compulsions of feeding and breeding.)

Is this a flagrant case of anthropomorphism? An abject instance of the pathetic fallacy? Well, I wouldn't be so quick to discount the experience of our fellow animals. Certainly, it's true that we don't know *for sure* if the eagle thrills in surfing the thermal vents, or if the turtle experiences a deep pleasure while basking in the sun.[8] But I find it more than likely that they do. Anyone who has spent quality time with a cat, dog, horse, or even cockatoo can vouch for the more-than-instinctual moments of pleasure in their creaturely companions — often gleaned by paying attention to specific facets of their environment. Many animals, after all, *play*, and play is a liminal mode of enjoying, testing, disassembling, simulating, stimulating, soliciting, and experimenting. It is a way of *being* (together) in a mode that goes beyond the blunt and mute fact of existing — or, indeed, beyond the biological imperative to procreate. We are thus much too quick when we presume consciousness or creativity to be present only in our own kind. Indeed, paying attention to *radically* different ways of being is one of the fastest, and most rewarding, ways to cultivate empathy with the world as a whole. Indeed, we can learn much from other critters. Imagine, for instance, experiencing a painting with the all-absorbing attention of a border collie stalking a stray sheep! Or picture receiving a piece of music with the intense immersion of an octopus receiving an enigmatic message described in vivid, flashing colors from a potential mate!

***

---

8   Alphonso Lingis, "Animal Body, Inhuman Face," Cary Wolfe, ed. *Zoontologies: The Question of the Animal* (Minneapolis: Minnesota UP, 2003).

"You are what you pay attention to."

This striking observation has been made at one time or another by theologians, chefs, and efficiency experts and forms the premise of this book. "Paying attention is an art and a practice that can be cultivated, learned, and relearned," writes historian Carla Nappi. "When done thoughtfully, paying attention transforms both the object and the giver of attention. It is a metamorphic practice."[9] In the previous pages, I offered a human menagerie — and not only human — of different ways of seeing, comprehending, assessing, interpreting, and responding to the world (ways that have settled over time into specific patterns, taught by one generation to the next).[10] After all, a fighter pilot notices very different things to an opera singer — even if they are sitting at the same table for the same dinner date. Similarly, a new urban courtyard will provoke or inspire different forms of perception and response when encountered by a landscape architect, a policeman, an office worker, a homeless person, and a skateboarder.[11]

---

9   Carla Nappi, *Translating Early Modern China: Illegible Cities* (Cambridge: Cambridge University Press, 2021), p. 5.

10   The most authoritative reference for the historical, cultural, and political forces which have shaped "the attention economy" in modern times is Jonathan Crary's *Suspensions of Perception: Attention, Spectacle, and Modern Culture* (Cambridge, MA: MIT Press, 2001).

11   It's true that two expert readers of Romantic Victorian poems may argue over the meaning of a specific word in a specific stanza with a vehemence incomprehensible to outsiders, taking the debate all the way to the grave if need be. However, the terms of engagement — and the overall frames or lenses through which

While we humans are born with more or less the same organic "hardware" for navigating the world into which we find ourselves so suddenly (some might even say so *rudely*) thrown, we are quickly loaded up with different psychosocial "software" — from the first language to shape our tongue, to the family rules and rituals we soon absorb, to the education we receive (via TV as much as school), up to the highly tailored technical training we receive as the price of entry into becoming a useful member of society (whether this be as a windfarm maintenance manager, a social worker, a supermarket shelf stocker, or a long-lunching "philanthropist").

Once again, "you are what you pay attention to." For instance, if you think about the act of thinking, then you are already well on your way to becoming a philosopher. (Descartes famously paid attention to himself with such unblinking intensity that he prompted a personal existential crisis, only managing to pull himself back out of the abyss by noticing that if there was something called "Descartes" to notice in the first place, then indeed he must exist!) Such are the perils and pleasures of philosophical attention. If you think about cakes all day, however, you may well be on the road to becoming a baker (or a food critic). The list, of course, is endless — especially since new ways of paying attention are being invented every day, as we can see with the cryptocurrency miner or the viral app influencer.

---

ones has such a debate in the first place — are set in place by the protocols of academia, hermeneutics, literary criticism, and so on. Such is the degree to which our own impressions, understandings, and personal battles, are pre-shaped, if not fully pre-scripted, by the codes, customs, and particular ways of doing things that precede us.

Harking back to Descartes for a moment, we each take our own more prosaic version of the cogito with us, which helps us trace out the boundaries of our own attention ecology[12] (that is to say, the intimately interconnected environment of our world, both in terms of practical behavior and the more abstract value system on which it depends). Attention is therefore not just an ecology but also an *economy*, and as such, it comes with incentives, solicitations, scarcities (real or engineered), and other overdetermined modes of interaction and exchange. (Notice, for instance, the extent to which an office underling is obliged to pay attention to the mood of her boss in contrast to the other way around.) The attention economy names all the ways our capacity to notice this, that, or the other can be bribed, bought, bartered, leased, given, thrown away, sold, or withdrawn from circulation. Advertising — one of the most significant inventions of the past few centuries — is essentially an enterprise concerned with the *industrial engineering of attention*. And in our hyper-commercial world, advertising has set the tone for almost all forms of relating to the world and to each other (to the extent that many of us feel we must become our own "brand" in order to be noticed at all). But just as the tentacles of capitalism probe the circumference of the planet — yet fail, despite their best efforts, to exhaust each and every facet of the world — the attention economy is nested inside a wider attention ecology,[13] and between these we can find both symbiosis and tension, complicity and resistance.

---

12 Yves Citton, *The Ecology of Attention* (Cambridge: Polity, 2017).

13 Photosynthesis, for example, does not rely on the stock market per se, even as the number of plants and trees on earth *does* largely depend on the whim of hedge fund managers.

For the polymath thinker Vilém Flusser, already mentioned above, "We live in two worlds: one that is given and the other that is provoked by the attention we pay to it."[14] One wonders, however, what forces could hold two such worlds apart for very long, or how we could really distinguish one from the other. For while it's true that we take most of the stimuli that tickles our senses for granted, it's also true that a scent (or a texture, or a flavor, or a sound, or an idea) can jolt us into a new appreciation or understanding of the world. On the whole, we tend to move through life in a way that leaves most things undisturbed and unexamined. The world is the background scenery of our own drama (or comedy). In short, we encounter the local space-time continuum, for the most part, in its default factory setting — as it has been presented to us since as far back as we can personally remember. We *also* know, however, that certain things — art, literature, philosophy, politics, love — can jolt us out of this default setting. These can inspire us to move through the world in a more active way, now taking account of elements that we may have previously considered only incidental, or completely inconsequential. Suddenly *the world* itself emerges as more meaningful, more significant, and more alive by virtue of the new "lenses" through which we view it.

This is precisely why attention can be such a liberating, powerful faculty or force when we discover that it's not simply a passive process — a decoding of information streams that rush toward us — but a skill or orientation with which we provoke new worlds into being (to use Flusser's suggestive word). If we concede that you are what you pay attention to —

14   Vilém Flusser, *Natural:Mind* (Minnesota: Univocal, 2013), pp. 67–68.

as we have already asserted several times — then you can also change yourself by paying attention differently or to different things. By the same token, you can change the world — or at least some aspect of the world — when you pay attention to things that passed completely unheeded before. (Think of how many activists, for example, embark on their mission after an unexpected encounter with something they had never really paid attention to before, but which suddenly took command of their consciousness — and thus, soon enough, their conscience.)

***

Before we bring this whole endeavor to an end, however, it may be useful to make a distinction between *phenomenology* and attention. The former describes the experience of experience itself. It focuses on the manifold, multisensory ways we process the world "*as such* as we move through space and time. "Phenomenology" literally means "the study of that which appears," and it is thus engaged with questions of perception, consciousness, and the structures of experience. Attention is part of the phenomenological concern, but it's not the whole story. This is to say, the body — any living body whatsoever — is fashioned with a specific *sensorium*, or capacity to sense and perceive that which appears. Insects, for instance, have antennae, dogs have an exquisite sense of smell, and humans have the five senses.[15] When the philosopher Thomas Nagel famously asked, "What's it like to be a bat?" he was curious about a certain shared, default mode of *batness*.

---

15   Scientists are likely to add to these as we discover more about our own physical systems.

He didn't ask, "What's it like to be Terry the Bat, in contrast to Preethi the Bat?" In posing his original question, Nagel was essentially testing the limits of phenomenology, which is very much a human endeavor, to possibly include the animal world (if only in the mode of speculation).

In any case, there is always a form of "species-being" — a specific biological and phenomenological orientation toward existence — that forms the substrate of any given individual act of attention. Phenomenological processing precedes, structures, enables, shapes, frames, and informs the *specific* attention economy of any given entity. Most humans, for instance, are born with a body naturally wired up to receive signals from the outside world in the form of sound waves, light waves, chemical signals, and textural pressures. In this way we translate the raw materials of the environment into what we call sound, vision, taste, smell, and touch. These in turn form the frame within which we paint the singular picture of our own experience. What's more, the senses determine the organization of that experience into some kind of narrative or conceptual coherence (a process to which we give the name "identity" or "orientation"). Often, we base our sense of self around things we pay attention to — literature, music, romance, financial gain, and so on. Alternatively (and at the same time), we similarly refine our identity according to what we *don't* pay attention to: politics, pornography, sport, feminism, and so forth.

This is all to say that attention, as a faculty and a resource, does not occur in a vacuum but is itself structured and influenced by the organs, systems, and modes in which we toggle and focus on specific noun-like objects (what the philosophers sometimes call "qualia"). Somewhat counter-intuitively, this shared mental-physiological continuum is what allows for so much variety in the types of attention-giving. Human neurodiversity affords different ways of attuning to — or paying heed to — the world, to the extent that individuals can forge their own self-tailored world, through autistic absorption, for instance, or idiosyncratic forms of synesthesia.[16] (We can, for instance, imagine an argument between two synesthesiacs about whether the word "Wednesday" is yellow or not, or whether the song "Bittersweet Symphony" by the Verve evokes the smell of doughnuts or fish curry.) This is another way of reminding ourselves that there isn't simply a passive, neutral, objective world "out there" that we individuals are born into and then subsequently pay attention to. As any artist, parent, teacher, or chef knows, the form and quality of your attention *substantively changes* the world and allows new microworlds to emerge. It is a *creative* act (which may in turn have destructive consequences).

There are thus as many "worlds" or environments — what the great biologist Jakob Johann von Uexküll called *Umwelten* — as there are capacities to perceive them, no matter how narrow or expansive the physiological aperture opening up to the Greater Outside. (The tick, for instance, is essentially unconscious until a whiff of butyric acid suddenly opens up a more centrifugal form of being.) Uexküll offers the example of an oak tree, which conveys different "tones" to different beings in the vicinity: a protection tone to the fox, a use tone to the forester, a danger tone to the little girl, and a

---

16 See Pooja Rangan, "'Having a Voice': Toward an Autistic Counterdiscourse of Documentary," in *Immediations: The Humanitarian Impulse in Documentary* (Durham: Duke University Press, 2017).

climbing tone to the squirrel.[17] From this perspective, it makes little sense to ask what the tree itself *is* outside these radically different ways of encountering it, approaching it, or even inhabiting it. There is thus no "world" independent from the countless microworlds that comprise this conceptual conceit or convenience: each separate Umwelt — each bubble of experience — is barely even conscious of the next, and yet they are nested together in a miraculous kind of cosmic harmony.

As if to prove the Lacanian point that "there is no sexual [or even sensual] relationship," even in the natural world, experiments have been conducted on frogs demonstrating that they only recognize an insect when it is presented at a certain angle — otherwise the poor amphibian doesn't realize dinner is right in front of its face. Perplexing, then, to reflect on what worldly manifestations are similarly moving about in *our* midst without being even subliminally perceived, let alone consciously noticed. At any rate, as humans we are — like all animals — influenced by environmental factors in unconscious ways, from pheromones, to ambient noises, to pollen, to pollution. Our various physiological systems, on a sliding scale from nervous to foolishly confident, are thus continually involved in parsing and navigating "sub-perceptual encounters," which hum below the surface of conscious engagement. Similarly, we swim rather obliviously in a cultural medium, analogous to the viscous media in which bacteria grow and evolve. And through this connecting plasma, we feel the spirit of the times — the Zeitgeist. Moods and feelings are communicated through the wires — both

---

17 Jakob Johann von Uexküll, *A Foray Into the Worlds of Animals and Humans* (Minnesota: University of Minnesota Press, 2010), pp. 126–132.

visible and invisible — that connect us. We become anxious *together* when bad news is announced, like the beginning of a pandemic. Or we become jubilant together when better tidings arrive, like when a tyrant is eventually deposed from high office. More often than not, we dwell in the blurred zone between *affect* (or "pre-personal perceptions") and *emotion* (the embodied feelings that we have relatively neatly labeled and placed in legible boxes: "anger," "fear," "excitement," and so on). As such, the human attention economy is firmly rooted in physiology, but it's also absolutely colonized by culture, ideology, psychology, and — perhaps most significantly of all — technology.

***

Indeed, technology is so ubiquitous today that we may legitimately consider it a prosthetic organ, as Marshall McLuhan famously proclaimed (the wheel being an extension of the foot, the camera an extension of the eye, and so on). Technology has both amplified and amputated our capacity for attention. It has augmented our focal powers a millionfold — slowing time down, for instance, so that we may see the mechanics of motion more clearly. But in doing so, it has alienated our own perception from its basis in the body. Thanks to tele-vision, tele-phones, tele-commuting — and other forms of action at a distance — we find ourselves here, there, everywhere, and nowhere. What's more, augmented attention has exponentially multiplied the quantity of things to potentially pay attention to. Suddenly virtual objects are everywhere, jostling for attention in the organic world.

Things aren't quite as simple, however, as celebrating attention and demonizing distraction, since these two terms are, historically speaking, slippery, dialectical, and — sometimes — even interchangeable. For example, it is presumed that attention is the opposite of distraction, but more often than not this is a game of semantics. In other words, we tend to call forms of attention we deem undesirable "distraction." Distraction is thus another name for the *wrong kind* of attention. Think of how a teacher will say a student is distracted by her phone, where in the student's mind she is paying *attention* to an important text message. (Indeed, the smartphone is simultaneously a distraction device *and* a hyper-focusing machine.)[18] Or think of how a friend may seem distracted when he is in fact preoccupied with the mysterious motivations of his absent paramour to the exclusion of everything else. There is thus an implicit value system, or even an ideological infrastructure, in the criteria we use to sort attention from distraction — since they both name different angles on the same perceptual economy. Moreover, it is the people with power, or those who unthinkingly enjoy supporting the people with power, who get to name what type of attention is valid and valuable and which is trivial, unwelcome, or even subversive.

Today we pathologize the incapacity to attend to the correct things in the correct way, going so far as to create new entries in the medical textbooks, as with so-called attention-deficit disorder.[19] Granted, a certain percentage of the population exhibits cognitive issues that negatively affect their social capacities, and can thus benefit from new

18   Dominic Pettman, *Infinite Distraction: Paying Attention to Social Media* (Cambridge: Polity, 2016).

19   Lawrence H. Diller, *The Last Normal Child: Essays on the Intersection of Kids, Culture, and Psychiatric Drugs* (London: Praeger, 2006).

medications. There is a broader concern, however, when ADHD (attention-deficit-hyperactive disorder) becomes a ready watchword in the popular lexicon simply to describe — and even self-diagnose — the individual effects of a culture *deliberately engineered* to pull everyone's attention in a thousand directions at once. (Multitasking, for instance, turns out to be an impossible myth, since the brain is designed to pay attention to one thing at a time — so when we think we are multitasking, we are in fact wearing out our neurological clutch, switching from one mental gear to another, over and over again.)[20]

Rather than dose our way, en masse, to greater global focus, perhaps we should pause and… well… *pay attention* to all the ways in which our attention ecology encourages (nay, demands!) a type of subjectivity that is ripe for distraction — from the first thing in the morning to the last thing at night (or the reverse if you happen to be on the nightshift). For while mindfulness, as a privileged form of wellness, seems to be in vogue, its articulation in popular culture, and in "the discourse," is little more than token compensation for a much more deeply rooted injunction to work one's self to the bone, often on pointless activities and for subsistence wages.[21]

***

20 Ilya Posin, "There is No Such Thing as Multitasking," *Forbes*, Jan 7, 2015. https://www.forbes.com/sites/ilyapozin/2015/01/07/theres-no-such-thing-as-multitasking/

21 Ronald Purser, *McMindfulness: How Mindfulness Became the New Capitalist Spirituality* (London: Watkins Media, 2019). See also David Graeber, *Bullshit Jobs* (New York: Simon & Schuster, 2018). This is not, however, to disparage the practice of meditation, which

Sometimes we pay attention happily, or at least willingly. Other times, attention is extracted from us like a tooth. Our attention can be coaxed, gently and quietly, or else it can be hijacked and held hostage. We sometimes feel mesmerized by something — a song, a sculpture, a person. Other times we feel we need to *work* to find the payoff for our dedicated time (though this can make such rewards all the sweeter, as with a difficult mathematical equation or a literary masterpiece that comes to us slowly, and with great difficulty, but then arrives with all the more joy for our having persevered in the journey).

I therefore invite the reader to take account of the special *tension within attention* that so many of the previous portraits embody, respond to, and maneuver around. Our attention can be relatively passive, involving a relaxing, an opening up, a general sensing. Or it can be more active, requiring a tensing of the muscles, the mind, and the will: a deliberate focusing. If this collection of sketches illustrates anything, it is that attention is not an organic facility that we are simply born with more or less of, but a deeply cultural endeavor. Our attention is elicited, encouraged, disciplined, and trained through many different channels, on many different frequencies, for many different purposes (many benign, and many others far less so). Moreover, through the ever-present ambient pressures of discourse, we are taught to pay attention to certain things, and to ignore many others. None of this is innocent or neutral.[22]

---

is one of the oldest technologies we have with which to pay attention to the process — we might even say the gift — of attention itself.

22 There is a kind of moral undertone, or ethical imperative, to any call to pay *more* attention, or *better* attention. Clearly, this is a goal or ideal we can never achieve, since no one person can possibly pay quality attention to everything that deserves it, especially under

Attention, in short, is never simply a given; it is the result of many competing interests, and thus involves a coaxing, a seduction, an evasion, a capturing, a resisting capture, a forging, an affordance, a repurposing, and so on. For every frame placed around an object, we either succumb to the pre-emptive focus — as with Plato's "strange prisoners," trapped in the cave — or we strain to see beyond the frame. This latter impulse is not only the origin of critical thinking, but also of political action.

In order to better appreciate the attention ecology in which we ourselves are enmeshed, it is important to get a sense of how different professions, orientations, roles, and subject-positions pay attention to the world. The portraits in this book are but a tentative step toward such an inventory, approached in the spirit of curiosity, compassion, and perhaps even potential collaboration.

---

the pressures and constraints of modern life. My sense is, however, that the more attention we pay to the attention economy itself — including and especially its limits, asymmetries, and aporias — the more interesting, and even inspiring, discoveries we'll make along the way. (Especially if we do this *together*, in a considered, collective way.)

Afterword: A Micro-Fable

In the current age, when the attention ecology is largely dictated by mobile technologies, we might hazard a neo-Platonic fable or allegory of our own. In this scenario, we are no longer trapped in a cave, unbeknownst to ourselves — hypnotized by the shadows of seductive forms flickering on the cave wall. Instead, we walk around outside, in the real world, but with pieces of the cave still ensconced in our pockets. These fragments of our former imprisonment have, over the millennia, been polished to such a degree that they function like a mirror or crystal ball. And so we take these shards out of our pockets and stare at them at every opportunity, looking for who knows what. Eventually, a small group of stone-watchers are inspired to throw away their shiny talismans and attempt to engage with the world. They wonder what it would be like to contemplate the stars above rather than the constellations reflected in their palms. This group of misfits seek to direct their attention more widely and capaciously, out toward the horizon itself. And so they call themselves the Fugals, for they cultivate a *centrifugal* orientation toward the world — deliberately swirling their selfhood out into the environment like a fisherman's net. The Fugals even hope to convince the others to join them (these they call the Petals, since they live life in such a way as to bring the world inside them, with a hoarding, centripetal force).

The fact of the matter is that this fable is still being written, traced in our own behavior and our own decisions. Whether the future belongs to the Fugals or the Petals — or a happy compromise between the two — is ultimately up to us and how well we teach the next generation to pay attention to the question of attention itself.

EMBRACING ALIENATION

WHY WE SHOULDN'T
TRY TO FIND OURSELVES

TODD MCGOWAN

The left traditionally views alienation as something to be resisted or overcome, but could it actually be the key to our emancipation?

In *Embracing Alienation*, Todd McGowan challenges conventional thinking, proposing that the effort to overcome alienation — whether through therapy, political revolution, or ecological harmony — is not a truly radical response to the current state of the world. Instead, McGowan argues, alienation is a fundamental part of existence and should be embraced as a source of power. Rather than striving for an ideal unalienated state, this provocative work calls for a redemption of alienation itself as a new existential and political program.

Order online from RepeaterBooks.com

CAPITALISM: A HORROR STORY

GOTHIC MARXISM AND THE DARK SIDE OF THE RADICAL IMAGINATION

JON GREENAWAY

What does it mean to see horror in capitalism? What can horror tell us about the state and nature of capitalism?

Blending film criticism, cultural theory, and philosophy, *Capitalism: A Horror Story* examines literature, film, and philosophy, from Frankenstein to contemporary cinema, delving into the socio-political function of the monster, the haunted nature of the digital world, and the inescapable horror of contemporary capitalist politics.

Revitalizing the tradition of Romantic anticapitalism and offering a "dark way of being red", *Capitalism: A Horror Story* argues for a Gothic Marxism, showing how we can find revolutionary hope in horror- a site of monstrous becoming that opens the door to a Utopian future.

Order online from

QUIT EVERYTHING

INTERPRETING DEPRESSION

FRANCO "BIFO" BERARDI

Depression is rife amongst young people the world over. But what if this isn't depression as we know it, but instead a reaction to the chaos and collapse of a seemingly unchangeable and unliveable future?

In *Quit Everything*, Franco Berardi argues that this "depression" is actually conscious or unconscious withdrawal of psychological energy and a dis-investment of desire that he defines instead as "desertion". A desertion from political participation, from the daily grind of capitalism, from the brutal reality of climate collapse, and from a society which offers nothing but chaos and pain. Berardi analyses why this desertion is on the rise and why more people are quitting everything in our age of political impotence and the rise of the far-right, asking if we can find some political hope in desertion amongst the ruins of a world on the brink of collapse.

Order online from RepeaterBooks.com

Steal As Much As You Can

HOW TO WIN THE CULTURE WARS
IN AN AGE OF AUSTERITY

Nathalie Olah

Austerity has created suffering for millions, as well a generation beset with financial insecurity and crisis. Yet our TV, film, music, art and literature have never looked so rich, or so posh. During a period of immense struggle, the experiences of the majority have been pushed to the margins of our collective culture by the legacy media and its satellite industries – making it hard, if not impossible, to challenge those in power.

Steal as Much as You Can is the story of how this happened, exploring the rise of affluence in mainstream storytelling, and the corrosive effects of neoliberal and postmodern culture. By rejecting the established routines of achieving prosperity – and encouraging us to steal what we can from the establishment routes along the way – it offers hope to a bright and brilliant generation whose potential has suffered under these circumstances.

REPEATER BOOKS

is dedicated to the creation of a new reality. The landscape of twenty-first-century arts and letters is faded and inert, riven by fashionable cynicism, egotistical self-reference and a nostalgia for the recent past. Repeater intends to add its voice to those movements that wish to enter history and assert control over its currents, gathering together scattered and isolated voices with those who have already called for an escape from Capitalist Realism. Our desire is to publish in every sphere and genre, combining vigorous dissent and a pragmatic willingness to succeed where messianic abstraction and quiescent co-option have stalled: abstention is not an option: we are alive and we don't agree.